Space Chase

Book 2:

Elizabeth

By Dr Joe

Elizabeth

By Dr Joseph Ireland

- Dr Joe -

Copyright © Dr Joe Ireland, 2019 www.drjoe.id.au
Cover design by Dr Joseph Ireland
National Archives of Australia Cataloguing-in-Publication entry

Author:	Ireland, Dr Joe.
Title:	Space Chase: Elizabeth
Series:	Space Chase
Imprint:	Dr Joe, the travelling Scientist
ISBN:	9780648494171
Date:	7 December 2019
Pages:	156
Size:	15.24 cm x 22.86 cm (6 x 9 in)

Target Audience: Young adult / Primary school.
BISAC: EDU029030   Education, teaching materials
Dewey Number: 813   F IRE
Lexile Number: 750

The moral right of the author has been asserted. No part of this publication may be reproduced, stored in, or introduced into a retrieval system, or transmitted, in any form, or by any means (electronic, mechanical, photocopying, recording or otherwise) without the prior written permission of the publisher. All rights reserved. However, reasonable portions of this work may be used for educative purposes (up to 1 chapter).

This is a work of fiction. All the names, characters, organisations, spell descriptions, and events portrayed in this book are products of the author's imagination. Any resemblance to any organisation, event or actual person (living or dead) is unintentional. Unless you are a sentient, advanced alien space ship masquerading as a twelve year old human female. Then, yes, this book is probably about you.

Cover art and Hovercraft by Nathan Clark
newnclark29@hotmail.com

Edited by www.adroitediting.com.au

To Lucinda Ireland –
   an angel on Earth.

To the Jackman family –
   and their inspiring zest for love, life and
   learning.

Originally published 2013 By Dr Joe. © Dr Joseph Ireland, 2013
   2nd edition published 2016 with Create Space © 2016
      ISBN: 9781530734078
   3rd edition 2019 with Lightning Spark © Dr Joseph Ireland
      ISBN: 9780648494171

© Joseph Ireland 2013
Feedback and comments welcome – www.DrJoe.id.au
Stylised picture of brain on spine taken 25 mar 2016 from
http://clipart.me/premium-people/brain-450696

Table of contents

Table of contents 6
Table of images 7
Introduction The scientist 12
Chapter 1 The day Mum returned 16
Chapter 2 The energy efficient house 25
Chapter 3 Lessons 32
Chapter 4 Good ideas 39
Chapter 5 Shoebox studies 45
Chapter 6 The experiment 52
Chapter 7 Market guests 65
Chapter 8 The P14 weather satellite 77
Chapter 9 The Trojan 88
Chapter 10 The second market 100
Chapter 11 Mum 110
Chapter 12 Visit from a scientist 118
Chapter 13 Battle for Arrendrallendriania 123
Chapter 14 Kharon 132
Chapter 15 Venus 139
Chapter 16 Ice in a Box 147
About the author 153

Table of images

1 Energy efficient houses 25
2 How to fix a satellite 81
3 A real live hovercraft 102

All footnotes are available as live links at

www.DrJoe.id.au

Make sure you check with your parent or guardian first.

More wonderful titles by Dr Joe & Creating Science:

Delightful high fantasy for the thoughtful young reader
   Choice, set free;
   1: The Quest of the Tae'anaryn
   2: The Tae'anaryn and the Wizard's Apprentice
   3: The Tae'anaryn and the Paladin's Squire
   4: The Tae'anaryn and the Enchantress's Chrysalis
   5: The Tae'anaryn and the Spear of the Troll Prince
   6: The Tae'anaryn and the Khozmoh Djinn

An engaging science fiction adventure that introduces real science concepts to readers.
   Space Chase 1: Arrendrallendriania
   Space Chase 2: Elizabeth
   Space Chase 3: Daniel
   Space Chase 4: The Mechanizer
   Space Chase 5: Moiya
   Space Chase 6: Pancake

Thrilling young adult science fantasy adventure.
   The Dragon Riders of Pearl
   The Dragon Riders of Pearl 2: Seven Worlds
   The Dragon Riders of Pearl 3: Return of the Plague
   The Dragon Riders of Pearl 4: Rage of the Dragonmen
   The Dragon Riders of Peart 5: Twilight of the Giants

And for the budding scientist:
   Creating Science – Dr Joe's book of science experiments and activities
   And
   Creating Science 2 – Dangerous Science!

Some important science concepts in the book:
- Heat transfer P.29
    - Conduction P.46
    - Radiation P.57
    - Convection P.87
- States of matter P.47
    - Advanced states of matter P.85
- Spectroscopy (colour and heat) P.84

Buy your own copy at www.DrJoe.id.au!

Introduction
The scientist

Cold laughter echoed around the abandoned military base as the scanner clicked as it turned over to one.

"You see, Obi! It worked, it worked!" the scientist screamed with maniacal glee.

Obi-jo said nothing. Obi-jo couldn't speak, but the scientist knew what she was thinking by the way she clapped her hands with joy. Obi-jo was a super intelligent orangutan she'd stolen from the secret biomedical research facility underneath Melbourne Zoo that almost nobody knew about. Oh, it was all right; after all, Obi-jo had had fragments of the scientist's own genius DNA implanted in her before birth, so in a sense, the great ape was *her* experiment, almost … family.

But no other human could reliably interpret the constant stream of numbers on the green screen the scientist was using, except Obi-jo. The orangutan had built the machine using old computer parts, secret files hacked from government websites, and stolen parts from the military research facility where the scientist worked. Where she *no longer* worked. Not since the accident, not since they found out what she was trying to do.

Her work had suffered a major setback then. But not now. Not today, the day the machine finally turned out a one.

"We've found one!" the scientist shouted again. All her work and research had finally paid off. "Oh, Obi, once I have proof, then they'll be *forced* to believe. Then they'll all see that I was *right*, and they'll have to apologise!"

Within a month, by her estimates, she would finally locate the alien vessel. After that the work would really begin. There would be the advanced alien computer systems for Obi-jo to translate, and then she herself would plunder it for the secrets that it held. Then there was the potential for working models of the technology that she could sell to further her research.

Then there was the dissection. She was looking forward to cutting up aliens the most; there was still so much she needed to learn their strange biology!

Her mind flashed back to a memory she tried so often to forget. She'd been there, when she was young, on their space ships. She was sure of it, from the nightmares she still had. She'd make them pay for the indignities they'd done to her and the humiliation she'd faced her whole life, living in a world that still refused to believe in creatures that no-one else had seen. She'd make *all* the aliens pay, and make her world safe once more. And then everyone would thank her and pour out tears of gratitude for saving them.

Obi-jo was talking, using the only language she could communicate with – Auslan sign language, *Triangulating co-ordinates of the positive indication of advanced alien shielding.*

"Hmm. Somewhere north of Byron Bay, south of Rockhampton," the scientist muttered, patting her ape with gratitude. Obi-jo leaned over as though expecting a hug, but the scientist pushed her out of her personal space without a second thought.

The scientist's fingers bashed on her keyboard. She used it to connect with the only other computer which could give them full access to the secret organisation of the Australian Government: ASIO.

She smiled to herself. They'd never found her, Obi-jo was too quick: too intelligent for them all! Using a complicated system of false identifications, bouncing her signal off several satellites, she hacked into the Cray supercomputer in Sydney and used it to invite herself into

ASIO head office. Using a web search engine of Obi-jo's personal design, she isolated key files in only seconds.

"Fascinating, what is a class two research and reclamation vessel?" The scientist mused while files downloaded like crazy to her computer. Suddenly a little electronic alarm sounded. "Tools! They're trying to hack our location!" she cursed.

Pull the plug, pull the plug! Obi-jo signed frantically.

"No, I've got this ... I can ..." She insisted, while the little green lights lit up, indicating someone was hacking back down their feed line which they'd twisted all around the Earth to disguise themselves. They'd never found her before.

But they were incredibly fast this time.

She could do this. Five lights ... then four ... three! The data only needed a second more. She could do this, she could –

Suddenly all the lights went dead, and the room went pitch black.

"Obi? Obi-jo?" she asked in the darkness.

A soft, furry hand found its way into hers and led her in the darkness to the emergency lighting. Obi-jo threw the emergency power switch. The scientist looked out at another disaster, a disaster which might have only just saved them both from being turned back into experiments ... again.

"Thanks, Obi," she muttered.

The orangutan hooted gently in what might have been agreement.

The scientist sighed, and her expression grew dark with determination once more. "This is only a minor setback. We have a location, so it looks like it's time to move again. Still, so many questions to answer, hey, Obi?"

She tied her messy black hair into a tight bun.

"Maybe it's time I called in a favour from the boys at the Federal Police again."

Chapter 1
The day Mum returned

Nothing could have prepared Chase for the surprise he got after arriving home. They'd just gotten back from defeating the school bully in a rocket contest, and Chase had never been happier: he was almost skipping.

His dad was at the front door and he was smiling too. But his smile quickly faded when he saw a black car pull up in front of their old, rundown house. Chase turned to see two tall men in dark suits get out. They were the Federal Police, or at least they'd always claimed to be the Federal Police. One was Flannigan, tall and lanky, quick to smile and even quicker to say something dumb. He had sandy hair and misbehaving eyes like he was supposed to be wearing glasses but never did.

The other man was Costa: shorter and darker skinned. He had no accent, yet looked like he was from Central America. And he was always angry, like at any moment he might pop out a big Cuban cigar and start puffing on it just so that he could blow obnoxious fumes into the faces of anyone he didn't like, which seemed to be about everyone. He was hard; tough as wrought iron and solid as steel, and he liked to show it.

But it was the third person getting out of the police car that caught Chase's interest the most. A woman: a neat, professional woman. Her hair was raven black, pulled back in a business-like bun. She stood up out of the driver's seat like a heartless executioner arriving at work. The air seemed to grow cold around her. She wore a porcelain smile, but there was no kindness in her eyes.

For a moment Chase couldn't say anything. She looked *just* like the woman in the old photos that were lying around the house. The woman with black hair and a ready smile, holding two twin boys as they played. The woman he once called mother.

"Elizabeth?" Dad stuttered in disbelief.

"Who's Elizabeth?" Arren asked.

Arren was Chase's friend, maybe his best friend. Only, the thing with Arren was that she wasn't actually human - which wasn't a problem, except they couldn't tell anyone. She was some kind of self-aware machine that was hiding from alien pirates who wanted to make her a slave again. They'd fought them off just a few days ago. Just like they'd fought off the Universal Unity who'd sent a huge silver robot to capture her. Just like they'd fought off the Federal Police who wanted to get their hands on her technology very, very badly.

The same Federal Police that were walking down the front path right now.

No-one said anything till they were all standing together at the front door. Arren was hiding at the back with Chase's dad. Between the two groups stood Chase and Lucky.

Lucky was Chase's kind but ... hyperactive twin brother, a classic class clown. He had reckless blond hair and disobedient freckles that splattered all over his arms, face, and eyelids. He didn't like book work, which was bad because he kept getting behind, even though he was every bit as clever as Chase when he applied himself. Trouble was, since Arren had given him some kind of alien make over last week Lucky was now like a pro footballer, super athlete and Olympic gymnast all in one. It was getting harder and harder to keep him from walking upside down on the monkey bars, or throw pencils to slay flies on the other side of the room. He loved to tease people, and almost always seemed happy.

On the other side of the open door were the Federal Police, and a woman who could only be their mother. A woman who they hadn't seen since they were four.

Only Chase found his voice enough to speak, the sound rasping out of disbelieving lungs. "Mum?"

"Hello boys, Darryl, and your *exchange student*. May we come in?" she said in a cold, business-like fashion.

Everyone looked at Darryl, Chase's dad, waiting for him to speak.

"I can't believe you ... you ... how *can* you come back like this?!" Dad said, sounding angry for the first time Chase could remember.

She smiled, but it was an artificial smile. "I don't have time to revisit the past with you Darryl. I am here on business, you know that," she said with a flat, unkind voice.

Dad looked down, like there was so much he wanted to say but just didn't know how. "You were always on business, weren't you Elizabeth, always caught up in your research. Fair enough then, I see we're not going to get you Feds off our property that easy. But I want you and your *friends* to promise first that you mean us no harm; that you're going to leave me, and the boys, and Arren our friend here in peace."

She cocked an eyebrow at him, like she didn't think his opinion mattered anyway. "We come with an offer of peace from the Australian Government, surely your... *illegal alien* would be interested in that?" she said. The phrase usually referred to people from other countries except in this case Arren really was an alien, and if you got specific about it, she really was here illegally too. "*Especially* if she intends to stay," she said, looking meaningfully over at Arren.

"Don't worry about them," Arren said and rested her hand on Dad's arm. "These police aren't armed and I can have us out of here before the two hiding in the taxi down the street can even get out of their car."

Flannigan raised his eyebrows at Costa in a kind of 'told you so' gesture, and Costa almost seemed mad enough to hit him.

Dad smiled. "Come on in then," he said with a confident grin.

They walked inside. Chase's hippy Dad had rediscovered cleaning since Arren had come to stay, but the house was still pretty much a mess, and it was very hard to tell the intentional disorganisation from the legitimate rubbish. Dad just was never very good at keeping house.

"See you still live like a pig," Mum muttered.

"And you still work like a dog," Dad mumbled.

They aren't getting along very well for their first visit in eight years, Chase thought. His first thought was to run up and hug his mother, but she had her arms folded as if everything, and everyone, in this place put her on edge. Like the last thing she ever wanted was to be touched. He felt a little angry, but also sorry for her, though he couldn't tell why. But most of all he was curious. Curious to know why she'd suddenly come back, curious to know why she'd left. Curious to know where she'd been for the past eight years.

Lucky, Chase and Arren sat on the sofa, Dad on the arm. Costa and Mum stood, while Flannigan tried to settle himself on the TV table and accidentally knocked over a whole pile of magazines Dad had only just semi-organised.

"Oops," Flannigan muttered, and tried to make like it didn't happen.

"Let's get right to business," Mum said in an impatient voice.

"Elizabeth," Dad interrupted, "where have you been? We've been missing you."

"I don't have the time or interest to discuss that with you now," she said flatly. "I am here on professional business. The fact that our pasts coincide is irrelevant to what must be done in the current situation. I ask you to remember that."

They were silent.

"Look," Flannigan said, "there'll be time to share stories later. For now, we've got work to do."

"Yes," said Mum, "and naturally it concerns you, young woman. Your name is Arren, I believe?"

"Actually, it's–" Chase began, always trying to get it right.

"It's Arren." Arren replied, putting her hand on his wrist to stop him.

Mum looked at that hand.

"Well, young Arren and you boys, the Australian Government is willing to renegotiate the terms of your stay in our country. However we are unimpressed, to say the *least*, regarding your cover story."

"Yeah!" Flannigan burst out. "What a load of–"

Mum silenced him with a single cold look.

"Your cover story of being an exchange student from France. It is pathetic, and wide full of holes. And you don't have any way of preventing anyone from seeing right through it."

They were silent.

"So, what do you plan to do about it?" Dad asked.

"I will do this," she said in her bossy monotone. "Arren, you are hereby invited to remain on Earth, in Australia, for as long as you like. You are granted a temporary citizenship visa, one of only a few in existence–"

"You mean there are others?" Chase interrupted, wondering if there were other aliens hiding in Australia.

His mum didn't answer him. "Furthermore, here is your French birth certificate, indicating you come from the town of Perliou, near the South, and are distantly related to this family by birth. Here are your first term results from the school that Chase and Lucky attend ..."

She was handing the papers towards Arren, placing them on the cluttered coffee table.

"They're all *lies*," Arren said, unimpressed. Arren, and apparently most of the rest of the universe, had a real problem with people who lied.

"Child, you don't have the luxury of your excessive moral values in the situation you have placed yourself," Mum lectured, sternness in her voice. It made Chase wonder, everything she said seemed to be designed to hurt or control someone. Perhaps that was why Dad let her leave? Or maybe she was the one hurting, and all the meanness was her way of keeping others away?

"Lies are still lies, regardless of *relative moralities*," Arren replied.

"People are curious on this world, Arren, and they will want to know. They will ask questions. And as soon as you hint that there is a part of your past that you don't want them to know, they will hunt it down. And when they find out what you are, there's no telling what they might feel the need to do."

"I'm not afraid," Arren said, poking out her chin.

"Nice of you to be preaching about secrets," Dad muttered to Mum.

"Just look at it this way," Flannigan abruptly cut in before people got any more upset. "Just keep the papers; it'll keep the school happy. Point is, you're invited here. You're welcome to stay here by those who've got the right to say whether you do or not! Just tell people you're from far away, that you had to run away, that you got a temporary visa to stay. *That's* all true, isn't it?"

Arren thought about that.

"You can let the boys do the lying for you," he continued.

But Chase knew Arren wouldn't let him lie for her. "Well, I can tell them you got a passport from France, and a temporary visa," he offered, since it was also true. But Arren tended to be the kind of 'allowing others to believe lies is as good as telling a lie' kind of person.

"Well," she finally said, "I am running away, and I am kind of like a refuge. And I do have your permission to stay here, as long as I want?"

"As long as you want," Mum replied in a bossy voice.

Suddenly Arren sat right up. "Birth certificate! Does that mean I can visit France?" she said, her voice just about glowing with enthusiasm.

Costa shook his head and buried his face in his palm.

But Mum held up her hands.

"It's a legitimate certificate Arren, though you may consider it a lie. The French government and we have a good understanding in such matters; it's not the first such arrangement we've had to negotiate. I wouldn't go there without *our* permission first though."

Arren nodded her head enthusiastically.

"Very well then, if it's all arranged." Mum nodded. "We've enrolled you properly in the school, which took a bit of work since you've been there for a week telling everyone you were on exchange."

Flannigan laughed, "That was such a thin lie, and I'd like to wring the neck of whoever thought of it!"

Lucky grinned.

"But it will do," Mum said.

"Wait a minute," Dad cut in. "What do *you* want? Why is the Australian Government doing all this?" He asked, leaning forward with interest. He was a great believer in conspiracy theories.

"Is it so hard to believe," Mum lectured, "that the Australian Government doesn't want to see a young girl, of *any* world, be returned to slavery? That we recognise that we overstepped our moral and legal obligations to all visitors to our shores last time we met?" She said, directing her last remark at Costa, who looked embarrassed. "That we are sorry, and that we believe a friendship based on mutual trust and respect will be more beneficial to us both than tearing this poor girl apart?"

"Yes!" Dad disagreed, shaking a pointed finger at them. "Yes, it *is* too difficult to believe!"

There was silence in the room for a moment, while the air seemed to sizzle with the electricity of their argument. Arguments neither Chase nor Lucky had ever heard when they were young.

Then Lucky spoke. "Mum, why'd you leave?" he suddenly asked.

She still looked angry at Dad for a moment, then softened. She looked around then, at Flannigan, like she wished they weren't around to hear.

"We had a lot of ... differences of opinion," Mum said.

"You still shouldn't have left," he replied.

She looked at him with a puzzled expression, like she didn't know what he meant, or what the logical answer to fix up this problem would be.

"Perhaps, but we'll have more time to talk later. I'm appointed to this case and I'm required to check in every week. Perhaps ... we can talk ..." she said, and smiled.

But it was the coldest, most artificial smile Chase had ever seen, and it sent chills all the way down his spine. He began to suspect that something was not right with her. That maybe ... maybe in leaving she was actually doing them a favour?

Then Dad blurted out, "You can't just walk in here and expect to start infecting our boys with your capitalist dogma!"

"I don't see how visiting my sons would be against the law," she said.

Dad glared, like there was a LOT more he wanted to say.

"Whatever," Dad finally said, without commitment. Maybe he thought he'd never win this argument anyway.

"Good. Then I expect to make my next call this time next week. Arren, was there anything else you'd like?"

She was silent.

"Very well. Boys?"

"Thank you for the permission for Arren to stay," Chase said, being polite.

"I'd like my life back," Lucky said. He sounded bitter.

Mum ignored him.

"Darryl?" she asked.

He was silent, and when he replied it was like they'd never been arguing at all. "Just an explanation," he said.

Mum was quiet for a bit. "Flannigan, Costa. I want you to go and wait in the car. I've some issues to discuss with the host of our national guest. Off record."

Costa paused as if to argue, but didn't. He walked out coldly. Lucky gave him a bright and cheeky smile because his brother could easily kick the Federal agent's butt if he wanted to, and they both knew it.

Dad and Mum went out the back of the house and talked in low voices for about ten minutes. Lucky went back to his computer games. Arren and Chase just waited, trying to read the paper. After that, the cold and hard woman they had once called mum left without a word.

Dad came in. "I'll fix dinner," was all he said.

Arren looked over at Chase. "Well, at least I get to stay," she said with a smile, finding something to be happy about in a very serious situation.

Chapter 2
The energy efficient house

1 Energy efficient houses

The competition was going to be fierce …

It started simply enough, it always did, but there was someone in Chase's science class that just didn't know how to take science projects lightly, especially when the opportunity to win came along. And that someone was Mark T.

"Here's what you have to do," the teacher explained. "Just as a house needs to keep people from extremes in temperature, you're going to learn about heat and insulation using a shoebox. So, using only materials around the house, and using nothing more than a shoe box, you are to keep an ice cube frozen for as long as possible. That's it[1]."

---

[1] Go online to www.drjoe.id.au to find instructions and examples for making your very own *Energy Efficient Shoebox*.

"That's it?" Mark T shouted. "So, like, what's the prize for winning?"

Mark T was the school bully. Seriously, even the other bullies were scared of him. He had a neck like a bull and probably weighed as much as one too. He was such a bully that some kids gave him their lunch money even when he didn't ask for it. Trouble was, he wasn't one of these dumb bullies who never got anywhere in life. He was smart, smarter than some of the teachers, and he let everyone know it. He was always bragging about how he'd broken into some military computers last year, and had the court summons to prove it. He told everyone he'd gotten off on some good behaviour deal being too young to prosecute[2]. But there was one thing Mark T was bad at – he was a bad looser. Just recently he'd lost the rocket contest and now he was out for revenge: and any reason to win was worth every effort in Mark T's book.

"Oh, there's no prize for winning ..." the teacher began, then scratched his chin like he was wrestling with a new idea in his brain, "except for the glory. Ooh, and maybe a handshake from the local council member when she visits next month!"

From that moment on, Chase knew; the competition was going to be *fierce*! Chase loved science because he loved to learn about the world. Not like Mark T, who loved science because it gave him a chance to prove he was smarter than everyone.

Well, almost everyone.

"No, you *idiot*," Mark T said to one of his lackeys in a loud whisper, "if you take the lid off it will heat up quicker."

---

[2] It is a famous misconception that someone is too young to prosecute or send to jail. You can get in very big trouble with the law, no matter what age you are.

"Naw, won't it need some way to let the heat out?" the lackey asked.

"That'll only work if the air outside is colder than the ice. I don't know any breezes around here that are below zero degrees[3]. Everything else will heat up the ice, *dork*!"

Really knows how to treat his friends, doesn't he? Chase thought.

"Oh, didn't think of that. What if we put something in there that's below zero degrees?" the lackey suggested.

"Not so loud!" Mark T chastened him, "Chase will hear!"

Chase had to smile; Mark T didn't bother him so much since he'd met Arren.

"So," Chase said to his two buddies, "how are we going to win this competition?"

"I wish we could use some thendretol[4]," Arren muttered.

"Can you really find that lying around your alien homes?" Lucky whispered, teasing her again.

She pushed him away. "Yeah, good point. But I really want to kick Mark T's butt!"

"I thought we weren't allowed to use any of your alien technology?" Chase said.

Arren looked like she really wanted to win, her pause worried him.

---

[3] Celsius, that is. Fahrenheit he would say 40 degrees. Pure water freezes when it gets cold enough, and that temperature is defined as 0 degrees Celsius. However, salt water will freeze at a different temperature, and that is defined as 0 degrees Fahrenheit. But in reality, 40 degrees Fahrenheit and 0 degrees centigrade are the same temperature, just different ways of measuring.

[4] A fantasy material I made up that is extremely good at insulating things. A thin sheet of it could keep you cosy during a winter night in Antarctica – you might even overheat! Expeditions to cold environments often use insulating foil in their sleeping bags and blankets to stay warm and alive. Now tell me; if you put a thick woolly coat on a snowman does it melt faster, or stay cold longer?

"Naw, we'll play by the rules," she said, and started shoving big wads of cotton wool into a shoe box.

"Hey, what's that for?" Lucky asked.

"It's to keep the ice cool," Arren replied.

"Won't all that wool heat it up?"

"No, what makes you think that?" Chase asked.

"Because when you put on a coat, you get warm," Lucky said.

Finally Chase knew where he was coming from. "No, it only keeps you warm because your body is making heat. The wool is a kind of insulation, and it stops heat moving from place to place. That's why a coat heats you up."

"True," Arren explained, "but nothing, nothing 'makes' cold. That's really important to get from the start. Cold is just the absence of heat. You can take away heat and it feels cold, but you can't take away cold to make things hot. Got that? We can't make more cold. We only want to stop the heat from getting to the ice. That's what the cotton wool does. It helps slow down the heat from getting into the ice."

"Then wouldn't a whole bunch of ice cubes keep it cold the longest?" Lucky asked.

"Hey, that's a great idea Lucky," Arren complemented him, then raised her hand for the teacher. "How many ice cubes do we get?"

"Only one, I know what you're thinking my fine French exchange student," the science teacher replied. "I know you find ice cubes around the house, but you only get one for this activity."

"So I guess all we can do is pack it with cotton to keep the heat out," Lucky said.

Arren nodded and packed in more cotton wool until the box was completely full.

"Umm," Lucky asked, "where are the people going to live?"

"What?" She demanded.

"The people, it's an energy efficient house right, keeping the ice cool? Where will the people live if you fill the thing with cotton wool?"

"They don't … it doesn't matter how much room you leave for the little imaginary people!" Arren said, getting frustrated.

Chase intervened. "Sir, do we need to leave any space for people to live?"

"What? Hmm?" The distracted teacher mumbled. "Yes of course, living requirements versus insulation requirements – a constant design challenge. Just keep the ice icy the longest."

"How are we supposed to win a contest with such arbitrary requirements?" Arren whispered in frustration.

Mark T laughed at her.

"How does cotton stop the heat getting in anyway?" Lucky asked.

"Oh, I'm so glad you asked. There are three ways heat travels and we need to find a way to stop the heat getting in for each of the three ways. The first way is conduction. Heat travels along a solid without any other noticeable change in the solid. The second way is –" she started.

Lucky groaned. "Isn't the teacher going to tell us this anyway?"

"Of course," Arren said, "I'm reading his notes for tomorrow."

"How are you doing that?" Chase asked.

"It's in his online notes."

"I didn't know you could hack into the schools computers." Lucky smiled.

She looked very serious. "I don't hack into other people's computers, Lucky. It's stealing. His notes were uploaded for anyone to read at the start of term. I don't steal," she said, looking angry.

"OK! Chill sister."

"Do you want to beat Mark T?" she asked him.

"Yup," he replied.

"Then listen up. Three ways. Think of them all. It might save your life one day. **Conduction** is when heat runs along a solid object, like how you touch a hot pot and the heat runs into your hands and it burns them. Ever done that?"

"I have," Chase muttered.

"Yeah." Lucky smiled. "He was like four and Dad was all like 'Don't touch the pot, Chase, it's hot', and Chase is just sitting there and I know he'd thinking 'But it doesn't *look* hot' and as soon as Dad turns his back, Chase is all like 'Owowow'! Sooo funny!"

"Yeah, felt pretty stupid," Chase agreed.

"Experimenting at such a young age," she smiled.

"Soo ... conduction?" He tried to change the topic away from his past embarrassments.

"Yes. **Convection** is number two and goes for liquids and gasses. Like how hot air rises, cold air falls. Same with liquids; hot liquids rise. Got it? So if we let air near the ice, the air will cool down and fall, and warmer air from above will replace it, melting the ice really fast."

"Yup," Chase agreed.

"Finally, **radiation**. Heat can travel by radiation, like the sun. There's no air in space, or solid or liquid objects as you guys measure it[5], so the heat gets to Earth by the sun's radiation. Like with a camp fire, even when the wind is blowing the other way and you're not touching the fire, you can still feel the heat by the radiation coming off it. Mostly infrared radiation, to be precise."

"Radiation?" Lucky said, looking worried.

---

[5] Light and radiation travel in waves. But waves, at least the ones we know of, always travel *through* something. Light, it seems, travels fastest through <u>nothing at all</u>, and that's a bit of a scientific mystery... (i.e., 'the Ether')

"Not nuclear radiation: heat radiation," Arren answered. "Sometimes I wish you Earthlings had two different names for two very different things![6] Just think of infrared light as an invisible colour that carries heat really well[7]. Every hot object is glowing with infrared light, even people. Ever seen night vision goggles? People are radiating heat all the time, even if you cannot see it."

"Oh. For a moment there I thought you were trying to tell me fires could give us radiation poisoning."

"Please, you *did not* think that," she said.

"Naw, sometimes you don't make sense, Arren!"

"You can talk, *Lucky*!"

"Oh, Lucky!" Mark T teased them, making Arren's voice sound all romantic, and students laughed.

The teacher glared at him.

The three of them bent their heads together.

"Let's *win* this!" Arren whispered.

---

[6] I'm with you Arren. For example 'energy' in science is a mathematical concept, while 'energy' in society usually refers to 'energy sources' such as coal and hydroelectricity. It can get very confusing, since scientific 'energy' cannot be created or destroyed, while societies 'energy' will one day run out if we're not careful! See also such confusing words as 'theory', and 'experiment' and 'hypothesis' – if you don't know what a word means, don't use it!

[7] Infrared radiation was discovered when scientist William Herschel, in around 1800, decided to stick a thermometer in a rainbow he'd made on his desk with a prism and ray of sunshine. What an amazing scientist! Who had ever thought of sticking a thermometer in a rainbow? Anyway, he found the temperature increased as he went from purple to red, but then in a second stroke of creative genius he went *beyond* red. There he discovered the hottest colour of all. He decided it was a colour of light his eye couldn't see, but it transmitted heat energy better than any other colour. We now call it 'infrared light' because it goes beyond red. Infrared light is invisible but it does all the things other colours do: it will reflect in a mirror, slow down and change direction in matter, and travel through space at the speed of light (about 300,000 kilometres per second).

Chapter 3
Lessons

After school they all went down to Ms Garibaldi's place: Chase, Arren, and a very quiet Lucky. It took them an extra five minutes because Lucky was walking so slowly, his head down, his arms by his side.

Finally Chase felt he just had to ask him what was wrong.

"Nothing," Lucky replied.

Which, Chase decided, meant *Everything, but I'm not ready to talk about it just yet.* He probably wasn't bothered by Mark T or anything, so it must have been the whole Mum issue. Chase decided to leave it, he'd be around to talk about it when Lucky was ready.

So they walked in silence.

Ms Garibaldi greeted them all affectionately with hugs and ginger cookies, chatting away happily to Arren who spoke fluent Italian. Being an alien spaceship had its advantages, Arren seemed to be able to learn any language in a few minutes right off the internet.

They sat out the back of her house on the little wrought iron table where they'd first all met. Well, more or less, as Ms Garibaldi was either unconscious or asleep at the time.

Chase got to his maths homework right away. Lucky picked the paint off the table while staring out into the disorganised junk in the yard. Arren absentmindedly fiddled with a clock she'd found among the garbage while chatting away with the old lady. In some ways Chase didn't know what was more amazing, Arren's ability to fly to alien worlds or her ability to listen to old ladies ramble. Both must take inhuman amounts of willpower. Ms Garibaldi was watching Arren with great interest.

"But you, you children," Ms Garibaldi finally said in her halting English. "Why you come fixing all Mrs Garibaldi's momenti, eh? You shoulda be a doing your homework like thisa young man!"

"Oh, I don't mind. I can do my homework later," Arren said.

"Seriously, she really can." Lucky agreed, Arren hardly slept.

"Stilla, this old stuff? Who needs it now? Just olda memories for an olda lady," Ms Garibaldi complained. Complaining seemed to be the way she talked.

"What, this?" Arren said in disbelief. "This works perfectly!" She said, and plonked the clock on the table. She gave the little pendulum a swing, and off it went.

Ms Garibaldi's hands went to her cheeks in surprise. "Santo Cielo, figlia! How to you is it done?"

Arren smiled. "The spring needed replacing, and that was easy. And the cogs were all dirty. But it wasn't really broken. Just needed some ... affection, that's all."

Ms Garibaldi stared at it, eyes wide. "But now I have a new clock. This olda this, who needsa this?"

"Old?" Arren said in disbelief. "It can't be more than ten years old. Why would you build a clock to last only ten years? That's just ridiculous. Here. Let me fix it up better than new. Then, you can sell it."

"Sell?" Ms Garibaldi asked.

"Si," Arren replied in Italian, "vendere."

"No, no, no." The old woman replied. "I not needa the money."

"I could," Lucky muttered.

"I could sell it for you," Arren said, "and you could use the money to visit Italy, just like you're always talking about."

Ms Garibaldi smiled, and patted her on the cheek. "We need mucha piu ... sell, for this I think!"

"Well," Arren said, "every bit counts."

"Hang on, Arren, where are you going to sell this?" Lucky suddenly cut in.

Chase tried to be helpful. "We could try eBay, or the local newspaper."

"How about a *market*?" Arren said. "I've been learning all about them. Every town should have a market where people can meet and sell the things they make themselves. It'd be wonderful!"

"Yeah, but where would we do that?" Lucky said, sounding unenthusiastic.

"We could use the school grounds," Chase said, happy to support Arren in whatever crazy new plan she decided they needed to be involved in.

"That's a great idea!" she agreed.

"It is not a great idea," Lucky disagreed.

"Lucky," Chase finally had had enough. "What's the *matter* with you?" It seemed he was disagreeing with everything everyone said just because he could.

Lucky kicked the dirt. "Nothing," he said, and walked off.

Still not time to talk, Chase reasoned.

"Well," Ms Garibaldi said, "I thinka it being a great idea. Molto great."

"Yes!" said Arren.

"How we going-" Chase began.

"Ouch!" Arren suddenly shouted.

"Sia bene, ragazza?" Ms Garibaldi asked her.

"Si, si," Arren nodded. "Signora Garibaldi, mi possa prendere un bichiere di aqua?" she asked.

"Cherto!" Ms Garibaldi replied, stumbling up and pottering off.

"What?" Chase asked.

Arren bent over and whispered conspiratorially, "I sent her to get me a drink. Chase, someone just pinged me, I mean, my spaceship."

"What does that mean?" he asked.

"They just, um, sent out a high frequency multi-dimensional beacon that will reflect off my ship's hull, revealing its direction and distance to them."

"Why would anyone do that?" he asked.

"To find out where I am," she said, unimpressed.

"Do you think it's the Federal Police?"

"Why would they do that, they already know where I am."

"Good point."

"I've moved the ship, actually just shifted it."

"You mean it's still here?" Chase asked.

"Sure, I pushed it away into another dimension. The only thing I can't move out is the door. It's still hiding inside the ground, just not interacting with the soil so that they're in the same place but not touching. If I did move the door into another dimension the whole craft may become unanchored and drift among other planes forever."

"Really?" Chase said. "Would ... will that hurt?" Arren was neurologically bonded to her ship. Actually, she was just a part of it.

"Well, no, it wouldn't hurt. But it would still be very, very bad. Terrifying. Imagine losing your whole arm, while it's still stuck on. How would that be?"

"Like pins and needles, I guess."

"Pins and needles?" she asked. "What do you mean? Doesn't it hurt when you stick pins and needles in your arms?"

"Ahh, yes," Chase said, "but it's just a phrase. It happens just after you go numb."

"Oh, that. Yes, cutting off blood circulation etc. Is that what you call it? Strange," she mused.

"OK," Chase said, "we're off topic here. You said you got pinged?"

"Yeah."

"And …"

"And I said 'yeah'. I guess it's nothing to worry about. Just some nut looking around. They might not have even been looking for me," she said without commitment.

But Chase could tell, and he knew because she'd been bothered enough to send Ms Garibaldi away so she could speak, something about this bothered Arren. Something bothered her very much.

***

Her cold laughter echoed through the abandoned military base, and the scientist grabbed her scanner with glee. "Brisbane, northern suburbs," she announced.

World War II had been relatively kind to Australia, at least compared to many other countries, but they'd still secretly prepared for an invasion. They'd built dozens of underground bases and forts, hidden in secret places all over the county. As time and peace had called away their resources to other areas, places like this had become forgotten, visited only once a month by a tired old security guard who checked the locks and dozed in the foyer for a few hours.

He was easy to avoid.

But if he was here today, he would have heard the laughter, followed by the sounds of someone hastily packing: bottles, cases, and what could only be guns.

A small orangutan swung up and asked what she was doing.

"Turns out those boys at the Federal Police were more than useless," the scientist muttered, "No idea, no commitment. They didn't tell me anything I could use."

At least they'd given her a head start, and now with a multidimensional scanning device that she and Obi-jo had made, she had a rough distance and direction. She had found one of the aliens. Now, it was only a matter of time till she had one of her own to dissect. Simply a matter of time …

Suddenly there was a thunderous knock at the door.

"Open up, it's the police!" a man's voice shouted.

She trembled.

Obi-jo ran to her hiding place.

But the scientist just sat there. *The police*, she thought. They weren't supposed to find her yet. They weren't supposed to see her here. She checked her computer, opening the satellite images. There were at least a dozen of them, surrounding the building on all sides.

A moment later a heavy blow sounded against the door as someone kicked it, and she jumped involuntarily. Again the foot struck the door, the noise echoing throughout the abandoned building.

Carefully she closed her laptop computer.

A moment later the heavy wood gave way, and four armed police rushed in. They surveyed the area dangerously but stopped when they saw her.

"We thought we might find you here," one of them said, seeming relieved.

"How … how did you find me?" she asked. There was a gentle shuffle as Obi-jo adjusted herself in the cupboard, but the police didn't seem to notice.

"We had you trailed," he said, putting away his gun. "Come on. It pains me to see you like this. We need to get you back."

He offered her his hand.

"How … how many did you bring?" she asked.

He didn't seem to like that question. "Come on, boss. Let's do this the easy way. Come on."

Her hands went numb and she tried desperately not to tremble. It wasn't his fault, but now he was a problem. A problem for her, for Obi-jo, and for the world she was trying to protect.

"OK," she said, head down, defeated.

He helped her up.

At just the right moment she dropped her pen, bouncing it off her foot so that it rolled under the desk.

"I got it," he offered.

"No, no, I got it," she protested.

She crouched down under the desk and slid on her specially modified bike helmet. Grabbing the pen she stood up.

He looked at her helmet. "Ah, you ready to go then?"

"Yes, officer *Flannigan*," she lied, and with a push of a button hidden under her desk, she blasted everyone in the room with a high frequency stunning pulse.

The police, and any in the building or surrounding area, were knocked unconscious immediately. Obi-jo ran out and started packing their things.

What are you waiting for? Obi-jo screamed in sign language. *Hurry!*

"First things first," she said, using a hypospray on the police in the room. "A short term memory inhibitor. None of them will remember what they've seen here. It's not their fault."

*Do we **really** have time for this?* Obe-jo asked her.

"We don't need to harm *them*," she replied, dosing the other three. "Done. We should have at least an hour. Now let's get our stuff and leave."

Chapter 4
ood ideas

By Wednesday, Lucky began to open up. He'd spent the whole week playing computer games instead of running amok like he used to, and even the teachers began to seem worried about his sudden silence. He sprung it on Chase and Arren on their way to school early that day, kicking the dirt while they walked ahead discussing energy efficient houses.

"What I don't get," he said suddenly, "is why she never wrote. Never sent us a letter or *anything*."

"You mean your mother?" Arren guessed.

He nodded.

"It does seem a bit weird, doesn't it?" Chase agreed. "And why would she be working for the Federal Police?"

"And when she finally does come back," Lucky said, actually upset, "there's not so much as a hug, or a 'Hi, how you been? Did you miss me?' It's all just right down to business."

"Lucky," Arren began, as if she was going to say it wasn't Mum's fault. But Chase stopped her so that Lucky could talk out his feelings.

"She didn't even ask how we were doing at school," Lucky whimpered.

"What did your Dad say about her?" Arren asked.

"Nothing," Lucky replied.

"Mum left when we were four, so I hardly remember her." Chase explained. "I never remember them fighting. But Dad went nuts after she left, and the house has never been clean since. Well, not since you came along," Chase said to Arren, grateful for the effect she'd had on their lives.

"Hmm," she said. "She does seem very committed to her work. That's not a bad thing."

"I wonder what she even does for work?" Lucky said, his voice strained, his eyes just a little teary.

"I think we need to have a talk to Dad," Chase said.

"Mmm," Lucky nodded in agreement.

"You don't suppose," Chase asked, "that she's, I don't know, not *well*, I mean on an emotional level?"

"Just because you're good at your job doesn't make you unwell," Arren answered.

"I know, it's just a feeling I get."

Lucky didn't answer.

Chase decided it was time to move on. "Anyway, enough of this, how's that plan for starting a market at school going Arren?"

"Wonderful!" she replied, content to change topic. "I'm seeing the school council this afternoon to try and convince them to give it a go. You guys want to come along with me?"

"Sure, why not?" Lucky grumbled. "You drag us along wherever you go."

Arren smiled her 'Lucky' smile, which meant she had no idea what Lucky was going on about again.

Chase was silent. He didn't like the idea that Lucky didn't enjoy their adventures with Arren; it could get them all in terrible trouble one day. But he was even more worried that a grumbly, pouting Lucky might be, well, *bad luck*.

***

Lucky sat in the corner, head down, not saying a thing.

Arren stood at the end of the table, facing the whole school council without a twitch of nervousness. She was explaining every compelling reason ever invented that a small metropolitan school should consider holding a monthly school market. There were school and community collaboration opportunities, fundraising opportunities, local business networking opportunities.

And slowly, but surely, she was losing them.

Chase looked out at their faces, locked into polite smiles while their minds where clearly elsewhere. He saw the problem right away. The council president wasn't paying attention, but it seemed to Chase that he left all the important decisions up to the school vice principal anyway. She, however, was looking concerned. She probably wasn't worried about the networking, or the community involvement, or even the money since the school would be getting some and that was *always* a good idea. She was probably worried about time. Simply time. Who had the time or organise all this? To take the phone calls? To check the local laws? To help people set up on the day? A market was a great idea, but who had the *time*?

And they'd never give that responsibility to a school aged girl, unless …

Chase interrupted. "You know," he said to the council, and they all took an unconscious breath as his words changed the mood in the room. "My dad has offered to do all the organising for this. He's a full time dad, and he's got loads of time on his hands[8]."

Everyone just sat there. Even Arren, though Chase had no idea what she was thinking.

The president turned to the vice principal. "Could be a good way to earn money."

She shook her finger, not so easily won.

---

[8] I'm sorry, I know full time parents rarely have 'loads of time on their hands'. Taking care of other people is a big commitment. I don't know where Chase gets this opinion from, it wasn't me!

"Even so, there will be extra cleaning for the school, and the risk of damage to school property on the weekends. I don't think the increase in school fees will cover that."

Arren started to speak. "At five per cent per transaction, and given local population and socioeconomic dynamics, the school is likely to earn over a thousand dollars ..."

She prattled on.

Chase just watched. This didn't seem natural, what the vice principal had said. Not the sort of thing she was worried about. The cleaners were there on Saturdays anyway, and people usually picked up after themselves, if reminded.

Then he noticed her make a furtive glace at the school librarian who was on the council. The librarian's husband was the head cleaner. He was old, and was not terribly well, but they both worked, so they must have needed the money.

Chase invited himself into the conversation and interrupted again, talking directly to the head librarian. "Ms Doubs-Greenshaven, do you think your husband could handle the extra work?"

She sat up quick. "Of course! We were thinking of taking another cleaning job, this could be a life saver, even if it's only once a month!"

Arren caught on quickly. "And accessing cleaning skills from within the school will still cost less than hiring extra help."

But it wasn't necessary. The vice principal had made up her mind as soon as she'd heard the old cleaner would be up to it. She waved her to silence.

"All right, Arren, I support this notion. If your host father is happy to run this, have him contact me as soon as possible. Does anyone else see a problem?"

They'd all listened to Arren talk for over forty minutes. None of them wanted to talk about it anymore.

"Good. Then onto the textbook orders for next year. Children, you are dismissed," she said.

***

The minute they were out the door Arren squealed with delight and jumped up and down. She grabbed Chase's hand and started running down the corridor even as the entire council's muffled laughter echoed out from behind their door. She dragged him around the corner, Lucky stubbing his feet after.

"Thanks Chase," she said. "I really needed you in there. Their heart rates were low and galvanic skin response[9] indicated a very low level of engagement. But you knew just what to say. Cool! We've got a market! We've got a MARKET!"

"Yay, you got a market," Lucky said with false enthusiasm.

She ignored him, and skipped down the stairs, singing:

> *Old Mac Donald had a market,*
> *E-I-E-I-O!*
> *And in the market he sold some clocks,*
> *E-I-E-I-O!*

"She's nuts." Lucky smiled.

Chase just laughed and they followed her home to break the news to his dad.

---

[9] Every part of the body can conduct electricity, some parts better than others. The outside of the skin can actually change its conductivity, due to sweating, depending on various factors such as your emotional state. Lying can often increase it, being relaxed or asleep helps to lower it. This is called the galvanic skin response and can be used to help determine one's emotional state.

***

Dad was at first surprised, then dubious, then finally excited about the market. In the end though, Arren arranged it so that he had almost nothing to do with the first market except where completely necessary. Arren just answered the phone and said, "He's not available right now, please leave a message." Which was honest, he was usually meditating, or reading, or walking around in circles in the back yard. Then she'd call back with her answer ten minutes later. What was really weird was how she could do it while doing something else. Like watching TV; her voice echoing down the phone line while the rest of her was complaining about the lack of recycling messages on the news.

But Chase was happy for her, he felt things were finally beginning to look up for Arrendrallendriania ...

Chapter 5
Shoebox studies

It was the orangutan who found it first.

"Very good, Obi-jo," the scientist muttered. They'd been searching the area for a week now. They'd rented an old house in the city where the 'ping' had occurred, but it had been a sleepless and frustrating week of searching, and there were no further pings. Either the aliens had moved on, or they were hiding very carefully now. She'd spoken to a few of the locals, but they'd never given her any *useful* information on where the alien was *actually* hiding. She'd run into a few of her old relatives, that had been embarrassing, but useless.

So now she'd have to do it the old fashioned way: Microwaves.

The local airport had a powerful microwave radio station for guiding planes. What most citizens did not know was that it was also used by the military to test for low range guided missiles, and that the scientist could use those microwaves to detect the large mass of an alien space craft parked somewhere in the suburb.

A massive alien space craft being piloted by an alien, no doubt masquerading as a human. Probably preparing for an invasion, laughing at inferior human technology, testing human psychology for weaknesses they could exploit when the main fleet arrived.

I've been there ... the scientist thought with such bitterness that it twisted her stomach into knots. Vengeful, hateful knots. She remembered only flashes of what had happened, but she remembered she was afraid.

Well, this time, they would be the ones afraid, when she ripped the skin off their faces to show the world what they were really like, what they were really after ...

A hairy, orange hand was pulling at her cuff.

She hadn't realised how quickly she was breathing.

"Not now, Obi," the scientist growled, annoyed at having her vengeful thoughts disturbed. "You see, you see here, we've got a noticeable disturbance in the electromagnetic field, like waves around a rock in a pond. There's something out there. And it's them. We're finally going find them this time."

Obi-jo gave what sounded like an approving hoot.

"Then they'll finally pay ..."

***

During the next week Arren spent so much time fixing things up for the market that she didn't have any time to work on the shoe box project. Chase, on the other hand, was so fixated on winning the project he didn't have any time to work on the market. Lucky just ignored everything. By Saturday, Arren was skipping around Ms Garibaldi's garden fixing things while Chase had a dozen shoe boxes all lined up along the old wicker chest, experimenting with what things kept ice frozen the longest.

"If you keep opening the lids you'll let the heat in," Lucky said. He was catching up on homework after being too distracted to try most of the week. But Mum was due on Monday, and that seemed to cheer him up a bit.

"I know," Chase replied, "but I'm experimenting here. I'm worried about the ground. We're doing the energy efficient house test on the veranda at school, right? Well, that veranda is made of concrete, and that concrete will have been out in the sun all morning. So I want to figure out which material to build the floor of the house out of. I've got polystyrene, a block of wood, gravel, lamb's wool and bed sheets. Which do you think will work best[10]?"

Lucky didn't answer, but asked instead, "How's heat going to get in through any of that stuff?"

"OK," Arren paused in her running around to answer with one of her little science lessons. "Here's one way to describe how heat works – jiggling particles[11]!"

She grabbed a plastic container full of ping pong balls. "Every particle is always in motion. The kind of particle they are determines their reaction to the heat. At low temperatures the particles are all stuck next to each other, we call that a solid." Here she let the bottle rest, the little ping pong particles gently jiggling but not moving around much.

"As temperature increases they become a liquid, with the particles all sliding around each other but still not moving around enough to break away." Now the container was shaking so that the little particles were sliding all over each other.

"And if there's enough heat they will break away and fly around freely – we call that a gas[12]!" Then she shook the container so hard the ping pong balls flew around madly.

Suddenly she brought the container to rest with a huff. "Now, let me ask you, if these ping pong balls in here were bouncing around enough, do you think they might start to break apart?"

"You'd probably break the container first, but yep," Chase agreed.

---

[10] Hmmm, what would you use?

[11] Check out some video's online. This old educational video is just great! Conduction is from time mark 10:30.

[12] It's worth remembering that not all substances can change state, going from a solid to a gas and back again. For example, heating paper doesn't make liquid paper, it just burns.

"And it happens to particles too. Make a gas hot enough and the atoms will begin to break down, ripping off their electrons and turning into a kind of glowing soup of positive and negative charges. That's called *plasma*, and most scientists think of plasma as *another* state of matter[13], one that comes after a gas. That's what lightning is, anyway[14]. And since the sun has a giant electromagnetic field caused by its charged particles, it's more accurate to call your sun a big ball of plasma, not a ball of fire."

She shook the container more and more until, with a grin, she accidentally or deliberately let it go and the whole bottle flew through the air to crash far away in the mess that was Ms Garibaldi's place. "That's the mechanical model of heat, created by count Rumford in 1798[15]."

"Really?" Chase asked.

"Yep," she replied. "So if you want to keep your ice cold you have to stop the heat energy from whatever the shoe box is sitting on from getting in and heating up the ice. This

---

[13] So we have four natural states of matter, from coldest to hottest: Solid, liquid, gas, plasma ... yet there are many more!

[14] Lightning: Most people think of lightning and sparks as being made of electricity, but the electricity is the part you *don't* see. As the invisible electricity travels through the air it heats the air up so much that it becomes plasma and glows. So the part you see is glowing air. Because hot air rises, lightning and sparks, if they stay around long enough, also rise. Gases don't conduct electricity very well and must usually be turned into plasma to conduct electricity.

[15] Although, to be fair, there is a lot more to the story than Count Rumford and a year! The mechanical model was battling for acceptance against an older and more popular theory called 'caloric', and it took many scientists over a hundred years to decide that the mechanical model was the better theory. For example, caloric was supposed to be an invisible fluid that made things hot the more caloric they held. But Count Rumford pointed out that when using a huge drill to make a cannon there was less and less cannon to collect the caloric, yet the whole thing tended to get hotter and hotter. He said that heat was not a substance, but was our experience of the jiggling of the particles within, which could be explained by a blunt and noisy drill bit, but not much by an invisible fluid called caloric. The debate went on for ages!

makes the particles of ice bounce around until they start to move freely, you call that melting. If they heat up too much the particles may even break away into the air completely, you call that evaporation[16]."

"Oh, I wondered why that happened, like how puddles shrink in the sunlight," Lucky said. "The little bits of water fly away and into the air."

"That's right," she said, and turned back to fixing things.

"Hey," Lucky then asked, "why don't we just put a mini refrigerator in there? Something that keeps cooling things down?"

"That would work," Chase agreed, "but then we need to keep putting electricity into it. So it's not very energy efficient."

"It'll take more energy to keep the ice cool than to insulate the whole shoe box." Arren pointed out, her voice slowly fading as she climbed into an old piano looking for pieces or repairing it.

"Yeah, teacher'd probably think we were cheating," Lucky said, then noticed Arren. "What do you suppose she is doing?" he wondered.

"I ... I don't know," Chase admitted.

She was mumbling something incoherent when suddenly she shouted, "Come here!"

Chase looked at Lucky, she sounded worried. Without hesitation they ran over.

"Aha," she shouted as soon as they arrived.

"Arren, are you all right?" Lucky said.

---

[16] And when a gas becomes a liquid we call it *condensation*, and when liquid becomes a solid we call that *freezing*. So a steel table leg is, at room temperature, technically 'frozen metal' - since each substance will freeze at different temperatures. Do you know what we call it when a solid becomes a gas without melting? *Sublimation*. At room temperature and pressure carbon dioxide does just that, turning from a white rock into a cloudy vapour. That's why it's called 'dry' ice – it doesn't melt!

"Got you," she said from somewhere deep inside the piano. "Aargh, help!"

Her legs kicked fiercely, trying to get her out. They reached in and helped her.

"What is it?" Chase said, a touch worried.

"This!" she said and held out a little metal piano peg. "I found you, you *mischievous* little piano peg, yes you are, yes you *are*."

"That's all?" Lucky said angrily and stalked off. He'd obviously thought it was something much more serious.

"What's his problem now?" she asked.

"Don't know," Chase replied, assuming it was still about Mum, or all the homework he needed to catch up on. "What you got there?"

"This, look at this! Now I can fix this whole piano up as good as new." Then she drew near, getting conspiratorial. "Though I might use a few little tricks to clean up the rust and strengthen the metal frame, nanomachines should do it. Shhh," she said, making him smile.

"You're going to sell a piano at the market?" he asked.

"Of course, why not," she said with a wide sweep of her arms. "This whole place is a miracle! It's a treasure wonderland! Look: pots and kettles, pianos and jars. You could fill a whole apartment complex with everything here. All this wonderful, useful stuff just needing a little love and fixing. Won't you help me, Chase? It's such fun to make things useful again!"

He had to smile. "OK, but we've got to get this competition won, right?"

She looked straight at him. "Oh yeah, I completely forgot. I was having too much fun. Use polystyrene, it has the highest specific heat capacity[17], due to the air pockets, of anything you've collected there."

"Really?"

"Really," she said, "now come and help me move this old treasure under cover, I need to get out the sander so we can give her a new coat of varnish!"

---

[17] <u>Specific heat capacity</u> is the amount of energy required to raise a particular substance by one degree in temperature. Different substances have different heat capacities. So while it takes a lot of energy to raise water by one degree, the same amount of energy will raise copper by three degrees (depending on lots other things as well, such as size, pressure and initial temperature).

Chapter 6
The experiment

That evening they sat facing mum and two Federal Police. One of the police looked stern; glaring out at them like they were being interrogated for terrorism. The other one looked bored.

And Mum sat there too, looking cold and professional.

"It's not like that," she explained, "you can understand my concern, as a mother, if not as a liaison assigned to your case. We need to know what you've done to Lucky."

Chase sat with Arren and his brother, and they looked at each other. Dad was sitting in a camping chair he'd dug up from somewhere and positioned himself between the two groups.

"So ..." Lucky said, "you want to *experiment* on me."

"No! You can't, you mustn't!" Arren said, clutching his cuff, brow furrowed with deep concern.

"What," Flannigan said, coming out of his day dreaming. "You afraid we're going to hurt him? It's not like they're going to cut him up or anything. They just want to run a few simple tests, scans, take blood or something. No pain or trouble at all, right, one I.C.[18]?" He looked over at Mum.

"That is correct," she said. "We have all the paperwork here so you know what tests to expect, Lucky. They are all non-invasive; MRI scans and the like. No dissections, which is what I gather your off world friend here fears, unless there is something you want to conceal from us?"

Arren sat back, but still looked like she didn't believe them. "You won't find anything," she replied.

---

[18] One IC stands for 'first in charge'.

Mum looked right back. "I don't know what you've done to my son, Arren, but if there is any long term danger, such as genetic malfunction or radiation poisoning, we have a right to know."

Arren snickered then turned to face him. "Lucky, you don't have to do this," she said.

Costa stood up straight and breathed in noisily. He looked angry at what she'd said.

"I don't ..." Lucky paused. "It's not going to do any harm, is it, Mum?" he asked.

"Not at all, son," she said, and smiled her terrifying, soulless smile.

Lucky was looking at the papers, flicking through them like he might have been reading them, but not spending long enough to learn anything useful.

"You've a right," Arren repeated, "The government can't legally force you to undergo any procedures you don't–"

"I'll do it," he said flatly.

Costa brightened visibly and Mum sighed in relief.

Dad just shook his head.

"You'll need to skip school tomorrow," she told him, "and no breakfast."

"Yep," Lucky said.

It was clear the decision was made.

Mum went on for a bit, asking Arren how school was, and asking Chase if he was enjoying life. Then the three Federal Police left, though Costa looked like he really wished it had been a real interrogation.

"Lucky ..." Dad said after they'd left, like he was trying to start a conversation but didn't know how.

"Hey," Lucky replied.

"You sure about this?"

Lucky sighed. "Arren, can you tell me what you did?"

She paused a moment then shook her head.

"Well, I'd still like to know. You don't know what it's like, Dad. It's like I just, I don't know, when I'm energetic it's like I'm unstoppable, but when I'm tired I just close my eyes and then it's morning. Sports are boring, they're never a challenge any more, and everyone's winded before I even begin to break a sweat. I want to see what I can do, but I just keep having to hold back. What can I do, Arren?"

"Hang on, keep it down," Dad insisted. "I'm sure the government will have this place bugged."

"It's all right," Arren told him. "I keep this house so closed that the government can't spy on us, or anyone. It's more secure here than the pentagon."

"Oh," was all he said.

"So, what can I do?" Lucky repeated.

"I don't really know." Arren told him, "The gold energy is pretty individual. Some people don't notice any physical difference at all, but I knew you would. It just brought out more of you. You ... you have to find out what it means yourself."

"Sounds like I could learn a thing or two from those cops," he muttered and went to bed.

They watched him leave.

"I just don't trust them," Dad said. "They'll tell him anything he'd like to hear right now. I bet they'll probably try to slip a mind controlling drug into his drink, or ask him to find a way to betray you, Arren. We just can't trust *any* of them."

"Wish we could keep an eye on Lucky tomorrow," Chase said.

Dad pulled a piece of paper from his pocket, scratched around on the coffee table for a pen, and wrote a date on it.

"Take this," he instructed.

It was an absentee note, now dated for tomorrow. 'My kids are feeling a bit under the weather today and I've given them a sick day. Please help them catch up on any homework they might have missed.'

"Gee, Mr Lucky and Chase's dad," Arren said, "that's ... helpful."

"Hang on, why'd you have that note written but not dated just sitting in your pocket?" Chase wondered.

"Just had a feeling you might be needing it soon," Dad explained.

"He's getting very good at that." Arren smiled.

***

The next day they said goodbye to Lucky then walked back to the living room like they were about to spend the rest of the day there.

"How are we going to keep a watch on Lucky?" Chase asked, wondering if maybe Arren was going to turn the TV into one of her 'hole in space' spy things.

"Watch? No, let's just tag along," she replied.

The next moment, the door to her spaceship began to materialise on the living room wall. Dad was watching this time, the look on his face a priceless mix of fear and awe.

"I snuck it through the walls," she explained.

"You ... wow," Dad said.

"You should come along," she told him with a smile.

"Ahh, no thanks. I truly feel the need to keep my feet on the soil of this world," he replied, and he seemed true to his word. Chase realised he'd never seen his father wear shoes, so flying in a spaceship that could enter other dimensions was, well, probably *not* the kind of experience he was looking for.

Chase jumped right in. "We'll be back as soon as we can," he promised.

Arren shut the door with a click, and the sonic sun shower washed over them. Then they raced over to the control room.

"Hey, check this out," Arren said, and the walls of the control room began to disappear. "They're still there," she explained, "but I'm letting the light shine through to this dimension, where we are. You're quite safe."

Chase hadn't realised how fast he was breathing. It was incredible, it was as if they were standing right there, flying along without moving their feet. They moved through the air as if on invisible wings, looking around at all the people below. He could still see the ship around him, but now he could see the outside world as well. It was such a nifty trick, he was sure it would come in handy.

They soon found Lucky. He was driving in the Federal Police car and they were heading towards the hospital. Arren had no trouble following them, and with the myriad of screens in her control room she could watch Lucky, Mum, and everyone else they came across. Mum was reading something and Lucky was looking at Mum a lot. Costa was staring sternly at the road while he drove, while Flannigan picked his nose.

"I think I know why he's doing this," Chase suddenly realised.

Arren gave him a querying look from her burgundy control chair.

"Lucky I mean. He's doing Mum a favour, trying to get to know her better and hoping she will maybe give him some answers."

She thought about that for a moment, then said, "I agree."

They flew on in silence, watching the black car pull up to the hospital. But instead of going through the main entrance the disguised police car headed towards the bottom of the car park and went in through a hidden section Chase didn't even know was there.

Arren's space ship was as big as a football field, covered with ladders, gang planks and irregularly shaped rooms. But all of that was hidden in a nearby dimension right now and didn't even touch the solid stone of the buildings. It was amazing. It looked just like they were floating along the corridor, right among Lucky and the Federal Police.

"This is so cool," Chase said, almost too impressed for words.

Arren seemed pleased.

They passed by a check point, then another one, then down a corridor past a high security area that had a guard with a rifle. He took retinal scans from everyone. Chase couldn't help wincing every time they floated through a wall or person.

Finally Lucky and the others entered a room where a glass wall protected half a dozen doctors and other white clad workers from the room full of sports equipment, weights, roman rings, and a treadmill. There was a myriad of medical equipment, and strange computers with bleepers, dials and lights.

First Costa introduced everyone, then things got very boring while the scientists fiddled with dials and notes, or attached electrodes to Lucky. Mum even left for an hour or two while they were setting up.

"Hey, check this out," Arren said in surprise. She was looking at the glass wall.

"What?" Chase replied.

"That's double glazed glass," she said, like it explained everything.

"And ..." he said, encouraging her.

"Well, your school project. You know how there are three ways that heat travels, right? What's the second way?"

"Convection[19]," Chase remembered.

"Yes, convection, like air and water currents. Hot air rises right? And then cold air pushes into the gap that's left. So every room on a cold day has a little current where the hot air rises around a person or heater, flows out along the roof, and then cools and falls, where it flows along the ground and fills up the gap left around the hot person: A convection current. The whole planet has convection currents; magma convection helps moves the continents, and air convection helps make up the weather."

"Cool."

"Hot and cool." She smiled. "And a cool ice cube in your shoebox will cool the nearby air. And cold air falls. Then warmer air moves into the gap that's left. That sets up a convection current that will heat up the ice more and more. So how do we prevent convection currents near our ice?"

"I suppose we need to keep the air from moving in the shoebox somehow?"

"And that's why polystyrene is such good heat insulator," she explained. "It has lots of trapped air bubbles so the air has almost nowhere to go[20]. But that's still not the best part. What about if we got rid of the air all together? What if we had two layers of glass, just like this here, and took away as much of the air as we could from between the glass sheets? Do you think that would be energy efficient?" she said.

He had to agree with that. "Sure. Then there would be no convection currents at all."

"That's the principle that keeps thermos flasks working, you know. Two layers of, say, metal with almost no air between them. It keeps convection currents from heating

---

[19] Check out www.DrJoe.id.au for video footage that helps explain convection and many other great science ideas.

[20] Wet suits use a similar principle, keeping the water trapped next to your skin instead of floating away and taking your heat with it!

cold things up as quickly, or from cooling hot things down as much."

Then Chase hit on a problem.

"How we gonna make that work in a shoe box?"

"I wish we could at least use a double glassed cup to hold the ice, that'd work the best. But somehow I don't think your teacher will let us do that. Besides, it might look suspicious if I forge a double glazed glass cup, even though it's *so easy.* Instead, how about we can put a double glazed window in the side. That'd look good. Seriously, a shoebox made of double glazed glass would heat up a lot slower than cardboard!"

"So we need to stop the air currents inside the box. Got it," he said. Chase walked up and tried to touch the impressive window but his hand passed right through. Maybe they should just fill his whole shoebox with polystyrene?

Then a man in a white lab coat walked up to the window, looked out at Lucky and stared right through Chase. Chase looked deep into his brown, unfocused eyes. He felt like a ghost.

"A quick mention," Arren whispered, dragging him to the side. "While they cannot see or hear us, they're still human. So be careful."

"What's that mean?" Chase wondered.

"We're still here," she explained, "but shifted. OK? Um ... we're still *actually* here. Like, have you ever got that weird feeling when someone is standing too close to you but you can't see them? That can happen here too, so try not to touch anyone. And you know how you can tell when someone is staring at you? Yes? Well, don't do that either[21]. Just ... try to think *invisible,* OK?"

---

[21] This is a little science fiction, can you really know if someone is staring at you? Possibly <u>not</u>.

"OK," Chase said, wondering if she probably shouldn't have told him to think invisible, it made him worry about *being* visible. Like trying to tell him *not* to think of ice cream. It is really, really hard to *not* think about ice cream when somebody tells you to *not* think about ice cream![22]

The scientists gave Lucky some special clothes to put on; some kind of full body swimming costume with hundreds of sensors inside it. It was his exact size. They made him do some exercises and were pretty impressed with all the bleeping and numbers their computers made. Then they put him on the treadmill and told him to run.

He was jogging on at a nice pace when the head doctor spoke to Mum; both were standing inside the glass room.

"Cardiovascular response is completely normal," the doctor said, "though he's sweating less than we'd expect[23]. We haven't found anything unusual yet."

"We shall see," she replied. "Lucky," she announced through the speaker, "run faster."

"Sure," he replied and picked up his pace. Faster and faster he ran. Then faster. Then faster. Soon, his legs were a blur of movement and the treadmill whined with the effort. He was drawing in huge, slow breaths.

"It's incredible," the doctor muttered, "that's over thirty kilometres an hour, and he's keeping it up longer than an Olympic athlete."

---

[22] This is known as Ironic process theory.

[23] How does sweating cool you down? When your body gets too hot it pushes water onto your skin. As the water evaporates and becomes a gas it takes a little of the heat with it, helping the rest of you stay cool. If you run out of water to sweat out it can be very bad; your body might overheat and you can die. So make sure you drink plenty of water on hot, sweaty days – and try keep out of the sun and in a nice breeze!

Evaporation also helps to keep ice cool: as some ice melts and evaporates it helps keep the rest of the ice cool, but it's usually not enough to keep the rest frozen for long, and since the rest of the room is still above freezing, the ice will turn into liquid a piece at a time until it all evaporates.

"Hmmm," Mum muttered, and then she spoke to him through the speaker again. "Lucky, are you all right?" she asked.

"Yup!" he huffed.

"Can you run faster?"

Lucky grinned, like he knew he was already breaking records. He threw himself into it, but his legs still kept up at the same pace.

"No faster?" she asked.

"I can!" he replied, "I can feel it in my legs, but … but I need a reason."

"I don't understand," she replied.

"A reason," he shouted, "my legs need a *reason* to run as a fast as they can!"

Mum didn't reply.

Suddenly Lucky got a determined look on his face, a look Chase had never seen before, except maybe when he was protecting little kids from bullies. It made Chase step back.

And then Lucky suddenly sped up. Faster and faster his legs went, pounding on the treadmill with such force it shuddered and began to wobble. But Lucky kept going faster and faster.

Without warning, the treadmill mat snapped with an enormous crack, and the whole thing broke apart. With a huge leap Lucky pushed off it just as it exploded. He went flying towards the double glazed glass wall and twisted around mid-air to hit it feet first, shattering both panes of glass into a billion pieces. The doctors yelled, Mum screamed and Costa whipped out a gun, eyes wide with fear.

Lucky burst out laughing and stood on the ground amid the broken glass, not a scratch on him.

***

From that point on they were even more determined, putting Lucky through even harder tests. They took a dozen blood tests, x-rays, and body scans. They got him to hold his breath, which he did for four minutes, then they taught him how to hold it for twenty. They made him stretch, twist, juggle and hold. They even took to throwing things at him from four directions, trying to work out how he could hear them all flying through the air.

Lucky was superhuman.

Their tests went long into the night. Finally the chief doctor, still too excited to remove all the broken glass from his hair, explained to Mum. "We've looked at everything, and we're still waiting for the results of some of these tests, but from what I can tell there is no obvious reason why your boy is able to do these things. It's as if he's just really, exceptionally, almost inhumanly healthy. I'd love to explore him more in the coming days."

"An offer I'd most gladly grant," she replied, loud enough for everyone in the room to hear, "but this young man has schooling to attend to, and we are committed to his wellbeing."

"Of course," the doctor stammered.

"Look into your current data for the time being. We will arrange future visits at the convenience of the boy," she replied.

He looked like he wanted to say more, but didn't.

"Costa, Flannigan," she said, "please take Lucky home."

"Yes, sir," Costa replied.

Lucky was still stretching his muscles after the big workout, and looked very sad when he realised Mum was not coming.

"You … you're not taking me home, Mum?" he asked.

She looked at him, and in a fleeting moment it seemed a tiny shred of sympathy crossed her brow. "Sorry, Lucky, but I have an important report to prepare tonight and several priority meetings to attend tomorrow. It is vital that I prepare."

"Sure, 'K," he muttered, but Chase knew his brother well enough to know it was anything but OK. He was hurt.

Lucky left with Costa and Flannigan, saying nothing all the way home.

***

Again the scientist cursed. All day, *all day*! A woman of her talents should not be wasting a whole day looking for something that could not be found. She slammed her laptop closed and shut off the scanner in frustration.

The signal had disappeared shortly after breakfast, and it was gone all day. The alien hadn't taken the bait, and not even with the 'ping' had she been able to narrow it down to a suburb or street. After getting so close, she was beginning to fear the alien might have detected her presence and left.

Obi-jo hooted from the back of the van. She was hacking into people's Wi-Fi and scanning their inboxes for keywords, such as alien. But it was late, and the scientist was tired. It had been a long, disappointing day and now they needed rest. They would try again tomorrow, scanning a different suburb. Tonight it was time for bed.

On their way out they drove past a strange little house covered with wind catches. There were little crystals hanging in every doorway and organised mess all over the lawn. The scientist briefly wondered what kind of people lived there, wondering if they were any relation to the people who owned the junkyard she'd mapped that lay right next to the school with the sign 'market this Saturday'. Then she wondered briefly if the alien would be interested in attending a school market. A black car drove past, with two men in the front and a boy in the back seat. Normal people living normal lives, never knowing what dangers lurked among them.

But the dangers would have to wait another night. They'd already waited for years and the scientist and her orangutan needed to rest.

Chapter 7
Market guests

The scientist snapped her goggles over her face, their unique polarising lens' guaranteed to protect her from any alien memory erasing technology. She pulled on her gloves and buttoned her lab coat all the way up.

"This is it," she told Obi-jo, "I can feel it."

This is what? The great ape signed to her, not entirely paying attention while studying the computer screens.

"We've been searching for a month. The echoes always happen around this area, but what we don't know is why. I can *feel* it. *This* is the day we find the alien," she promised, testing her taser was fully charged once more.

***

By gosh I'm happy! Chase thought as he looked out at the bright, colourful stalls all over the oval. The day of the first market was finally here and everyone seemed to be having a great time. Mr Rowly, dad of one of the kids in his class, had started up a tool importing business from Asia and was ecstatic to have a place to sell. The local quilting club were there in force, and someone even talked them into offering classes at the school on weekends. The kids from the music department were taking turns at busking to raise money for more music, and Chase thought they actually sounded pretty decent.

Best of all, Dad was getting right into things as the man making it happen. Arren had filled him in on all the details, and he made a point of visiting every stall and speaking to every stallholder, calling them by name and shaking their hands. Chase hadn't seen him this excited in years.

He looked over, and it seemed Arren's piano was being sold for over five hundred dollars. They gave all they could to Ms Garibaldi who couldn't hide her tears of gratitude. She hadn't been back to Italy in forty years, and really wanted to see her country before she got too old to try.

"It'll still take almost a year to raise enough money to see her off." Arren said with a frown.

"Don't worry, there's plenty of things to fix!" Chase quoted her.

Just then some crazed grade four kids scurried past, chasing each other with ribbons on sticks. Some poor girl looked like she was 'it', and was probably 'it' quite often. She paused when she saw Arren and Chase looking at her.

"How's it going?" Arren asked.

"I wish there were some rides," she said randomly and ran off.

"What was that?" Chase laughed.

"Hmmm, rides ..." Arren muttered, "then we could charge two dollars per ride and keep it up all day!"

"What are you planning?" Chase asked.

"Nothing, just ... thinking," she said. Arren mightn't lie, but she sure could keep a secret.

***

"Bingo!"

Anyone walking beside the unmarked orange van would have heard the screams of elation and wondered what on earth was going on inside the beat-up old VW. But they could not have seen inside the blackened out windows, or heard what was being said.

The scientist spoke to herself, just loud enough so that Obi-jo would hear. She liked letting Obi-jo know what she was thinking. Together, they were pressed up tightly in the enclosed space of the van between a dozen computers, scanners, and other machines too mysterious to explain.

"There," the scientist said, "there, in the school fair. After all this time. I *knew* we'd find them today. But look, look at this! There's an image on the scanner, something huge is floating over the school grounds, almost as big as the entire school!"

It's them, isn't it? Obi-jo signed.

"Of course it is! Finally! I was afraid we'd lost them forever."

But what are they doing at a school fete? Obi-jo asked.

"I don't ... what does it matter?" the scientist almost shouted in a husky whisper. "I'm going in there, I'm–"

Obi-jo clung onto her cuff like it was her life line.

Obi-jo, her greatest creation, together they were misfits rejected from their own civilisation. A civilisation they were trying to protect. The scientist knew that if anything happened to herself, Obi-jo would have nowhere to go.

But there were questions that needed to be answered.

"I'll be all right," she insisted, hiding her own nervousness behind a bossy, professional voice. "I've been waiting for this all my life. I'm going in there, and I'm going to find the aliens."

Then what? Obi-jo signed.

"Track it to their lair, disable them, and show the whole world!"

A minute later she stumbled from the van in her old lab coat. She knew her unwashed trackies would do nothing to neaten up her appearance, but didn't care. Deep in her pockets she hid her high level scanning devices, filled with technologies most people on Earth weren't aware existed. Her thoughts were protected by the aluminium lined bike helmet she knew much better than to take off.

It was revelation time.

***

Chase laughed. Arren had somehow found two old socks at a stall and was entertaining some small children with a ridiculous rendition of *The Three Little Pigs*. They seemed to be very violent pigs, and it looked like the wolf was going to come to a very gruesome end.

Then something strange happened. It was just as if someone tapped Chase on the shoulder, like they were trying to get his attention. He didn't *feel* anything on his skin, yet suddenly he found himself very nervous. He looked around, wondering if he'd imagined it, or maybe it was just a random twitch or something.

Weird.

"Then they put the lid on the boiling pot and got out their *soup spoons*," Arren said.

"Ewww!" the children chorused, except for one boy who cheered.

Chase laughed. Arren was priceless, always making people laugh.

***

The scientist peered through the branches. The school was just at the bottom of a gentle hill, the market covering the largest field. Parents and their children scurried around the market grounds like ants, scrounging for scraps of food or meaningless bargains. They had no idea how much danger they were in. No idea at *all*.

Only *she* could see what was *really* happening as she looked through her high powered theroscopic microwave indulcement goggles[24]. They had used these back at the

---

[24] What now? Sounds like pure sci fi to me!

research base, but only she was smart enough to make them into goggles.

Peering intently into the goggles the scientist could see something, and it was huge; almost larger than the school market altogether. It was floating just above … no … it was resting on the ground. It was touching the earth but people were moving in and around it like they had no idea it was there. Well, anyone looking from above might have noticed the odd way in which people seemed to arrange their stalls in the exact same shape as the alien monstrosity, but none of them would have known why.

The scientist pushed herself deeper into the underbrush. It was impossible to tell, even from this distance, if the aliens had any way of knowing that she was there. Her helmet coating was the cheapest and most effective way of keeping out their alien mind reading abilities[25]. But they still might have some way of knowing she was there.

She peeped at her iPhone so that Obi-jo could sign to her.

*You're not thinking of going **in** there, are you?* Obi-jo looked worried.

Where else? she signed back. The aliens might not have a way to find her, but she definitely had a way to find them. A little device borrowed from the boys at the Federal Police. It looked like a little black rod: a scanning device. Built from stolen alien technology, it was so powerful that it could name and number every kind of atom in someone's body. But its most useful ability today was that it could tell exactly

---

[25] Do metal lined helmets prevent alien mind control and mind reading abilities? Given that we can't even tell, for now, if telepathy or aliens are real, it's an almost impossible task to scientifically know if the helmets help or not. But some, such as Michael Menkin, are convinced they do. Others, sometimes quite cynically at times, are sceptical that the improvements are nothing more than the placebo effect at best.

whether those atoms belonged to this earth or someone else's because of their quantum spin factors[26]. And it was this device that would tell her exactly who the aliens were, and then she would find a way to capture one and learn all about it – piece by piece.

***

"Careful!" Dad said, unnecessarily.

"I am being careful," Chase reassured him. They were carrying a large box. Some guy at the stall had seen Dad around and asked for his help. Then Dad had seen Chase and so now Chase was helping too.

"Cool, trackies." Arren smiled.

"Why do they weight so much?" Chase asked.

"There's quite a lot of thread in there."

"I didn't know thread could weigh so much," he complained.

"It's insulation. The threads inside keep the air trapped near the skin, and–"

"Oh, Chase dear," a voice called. It was Ms Doubs-Greenshaven, cleaner turned candy maker, busy working the fairy floss machine for a long line of little ballerinas in tutus.

"Be a dear," she said, "I just need a trip to the little girls' room. Can you please take over for a moment here, Chase?"

He didn't see any reason why he shouldn't, so he put down the box to help.

***

Nothing, nothing, nothing.

---

[26] This rod and its abilities are all made up, just in case you wondered.

She'd been at it for an hour, yet it seemed there wasn't a single alien there, even though their ship was resting right in the middle of the oval. The ship itself, of course, was shifted out into another dimension so that its molecules didn't react to the scanner. But even so, the scientist worried, it was as if the aliens weren't here at all.

Unless ... unless they were abducting people right under everyone's noses! Maybe there was a tent, like a palm reader or something and when people came along to get read their fortune, the poor fools got more than they'd paid for.

Suddenly her scanner gave an unexpected beep.

Carefully, from behind her coat, she swung her scanner around for another sweep. It beeped again. It was a boy, a boy who was smiling happily and handing out fairy floss to little ballerinas.

Of course! The perfect disguise!

She hid among some gaudy wind catchers at a crowded stall and popped out her computer, breathing heavily. This was it. This was ...

Point zero, zero two percent? *This was disappointing.* The total amount could not be more than a few grams of his body. Maybe less! How could he be the alien?

Maybe he'd been on their ship, and had some alien lunch recently? Or maybe there was an alien parasite infecting his body; controlling him like some kind of doll! Or more likely the aliens were slowly converting his body into their horrible alien life form, digesting him from the inside out as they grew!

She looked at him in pity, taking a few quick photos for further study. But a real alien had to be here somewhere. And did he know them?

As if on cue he looked up at another young girl about his age, with curly long hair and tanned skin, talking to a man in a business suit ...

And the scientist almost dropped her scanner as it gave an enormous PING.

Bingo!

I've found the alien, she cheered silently.

***

Chase was wrapping the melted pink sugar around a small stick when he looked up to see Arren chatting with the vice principal about how well the day was going.

And then, for no reason he could think of, he looked over to see a strangely dressed woman among some wind catchers at a nearby stall. Something about her made his hair stand on end. It wasn't the fact that she was wearing a strange bike helmet covered in foil, or even the incredibly messy lab coat she was wearing on a warm summer's day. It wasn't even the sneaky way she was looking at Arren while hiding behind a messy collection of hanging wind catchers.

Matter of fact, he couldn't put his finger on anything at all. She just made him feel really, really nervous.

"Hey!" the kid he was making fairy floss for suddenly shouted. Chase looked down to find the stick, his hand, and most of his forearm overflowing with crystallised sugar.

"Sorry," he muttered, and wiped the fairy floss from his arm[27]. Grabbing a new stick he looked up again.

But the weird looking woman was gone.

---

[27] Fairy floss, or cotton candy to the Americans, has been around for a long time. The modern method was initially invented by Wharton (a confectioner) and Morrison (ironically, a dentist) in around 1899. It works by melting sugar in a funnel, then flinging the sugar around using a spinning device called a centrifuge. This flinging cools the sugar so quickly it doesn't have time to crystallise again, and instead forms the long, silky threads we love to eat! And just in case you were wondering, fairy floss is more than 99% sugar – some kinds of *sugar* have less sugar than fairy floss!

It was weird. He didn't have any reason to be worried about the dark haired woman, but he was. More worried than if he'd met Mark T in a dark alley on a spooky night. But there was nothing he could do about it.

So she was dressed a little weird, there's nothing wrong with that. Brisbane is full of weird people, he thought. So he just shrugged his shoulders and forgot about it.

Arren walked over as soon as she'd finished talking to the vice principal.

"I wonder what Lucky's up to?" she asked him.

"I don't know, he should be around here somewhere."

"He's over there," she replied.

"Well if you know where he is, why are you wondering what he's up to?" Chase asked.

"His body temperature is up."

"How do you know that?"

"Oh, I've got my eye on things here," she said with a smile, and ran off in the direction she'd pointed.

Chase followed and found Lucky half a minute later, having a heated argument with someone selling food.

"It's all rubbish," Lucky said, almost shouting.

"Well if you don't like my food you can shove off young man," the seller said with an angry voice. Lucky and he had obviously been arguing for a while.

"Look, all I wanted to know was if you had anything *worth* eating!" Lucky replied.

"And I told you my *entire inventory!*" the guy shouted.

"Hey, Lucky!" Chase interrupted them.

Lucky turned and looked at him, and Chase realised Arren had probably brought him here to help diffuse things. Lucky usually didn't listen to her as much as he did to his twin.

He started stalking off as soon as he saw Arren, but they soon caught up.

"What's up?" Chase asked.

Lucky huffed, but turned around like he was glad to have someone to share his frustration with. "Look, I just wanted something to eat."

"Why didn't you get some chips?"

"Didn't like the smell. They smelt like they were soaked in oil."

"They are soaked in oil," Arren answered him. "That's how they cook them."

"Really? I mean, all the way?"

"Yes." She smiled.

"How about hot dogs?" Chase asked. "You always liked hot dogs."

"Yeah," Lucky smiled, "but they looked, I don't know, they just smelt old. Do you know what I mean? I wonder how long they keep them for?"

"They can be in cold storage for months before they're used," Arren claimed.

"Really?" Lucky asked, looking disgusted.

"So, what *do* you want to eat?" Chase asked.

"I don't know!" he replied. "This wasn't something you did to me, was it Arren?"

She shrugged.

"Just, hey, what's that?" Lucky said, stopping.

"What?" Arren asked.

"That ... smell ..."

"What smell?" Chase said.

"I cannot discern which is the scent to which you refer," Arren replied with a cheeky grin.

"That scent ..." Lucky said, walking off, sniffing the air.

Arren shook her head, and Chase shrugged. Together they followed Lucky.

"Arren," Chase asked her in private, "is it something you did?"

Arren smiled. "Adjusting to the changes does take time and it's very personal. It might be part of his way of expressing it, but I don't know. I guess I'm just tagging along, making sure nothing gets out of hand. You know Lucky."

Chase gulped down his nervousness. Oh yes, he knew Lucky all right. Once, when he'd been angry at a teacher he claimed had gotten him into trouble for nothing at all, he'd let all the air out of his tyres and then hidden under the car to see what would happen. Boy, did he get in trouble for that! Yes, Chase knew Lucky all right.

They ran to catch up but Lucky had stopped.

Right in the middle of the market garden.

"It's here," he said.

"What?" Chase asked.

Lucky walked along the neat rows of plants, pushing the leaves with his hands as he went along, breathing in deeply.

He was being very weird.

"This one," Lucky finally said. He was holding a big, fat leafy plant, one of several in a large dirty crate. He bent down, and sniffed the leaves deeply.

"Oh, yes," Lucky said with a grin.

"Well, um, if you're hungry I hope it's edi-" Chase began, then noticed Lucky had already taken a huge bite out of one of the leaves.

"Hey!" Lucky shouted at the store keeper, almost sounding angry. "Whatcha call this stuff!"

"Lettuce," he replied as Lucky began scoffing down leaves. "Hey, I hope you're planning to pay for that!"

"Oh," Lucky said, looking like the thought had only just occurred to him. "Yeah, how much?"

"One dollar."

Lucky almost choked. "But that's half as much as a hot dog!"

"Then you can buy two," the man grinned.

Lucky's smile got bigger.

Chase watched in wonder as his brother proceeded to try out every edible plant there, then spend his entire pocket money on seedlings to take home. Lucky didn't even seem to notice the rest of the day pass as he and the man discussed how to make them grow. Most of the stalls had closed by the time Dad could pull Lucky away. Dad had always had a love of pot plants, mostly flowers and herbs, so Lucky and Dad talked excitedly all the way home.

In so many ways, thought Chase, *a very good day.*

***

The scientist flung herself into the VW.

"After all this time ..." she muttered to herself, making sure Obi-jo was close enough to hear.

She'd seen her: the alien.

The scientist began downloading the data from her scanner, hoping the aliens hadn't detected her presence or remembered her. It was too dangerous. She and Obi-jo would have to be more careful from here on in.

So ... a girl. One of the aliens was pretending to be a girl, and a school girl at that. Strange indeed, what was she hiding from? Or was she hiding some secret inside herself?

But it didn't matter. Soon she'd be in her clutches. Then they'd all find out what she was *really* made of ...

... and what was *really* inside her ...

Chapter 8
The P14 weather satellite

That evening, after they'd made hundreds of dollars at the first market, Mum was waiting for them at home, and she made it clear she expecting a favour from Arren.

Arren was livid. "You can't ... no! I'll not do it!"

Mum was unimpressed. "Arren, it's not like we haven't been lenient with you," she began.

Flannigan cut her off. "'Sides, it's just a check-up," he said, his voice cheery. "A little weather satellite has stopped responding to calls and we need to know why, and see if maybe you can patch it up for us? Loads of people are relying on that satellite for their weather reports: farmers, aeroplane pilots ..."

Arren glared at him, like she knew he was trying to make her feel guilty. "Listen," she explained, looking exasperated. "I can't, even if I wanted to. The Universal Unity-"

"Have allowed you to be placed under our care, and as a ward of our care we have the right to request any services you are reasonably able to provide," Mum insisted, her voice formal and cold.

"Well," Arren replied, stomping her feet with emphasis. "Request denied."

Mum sighed. "I hoped it wouldn't come to this. You see, Arren, the monthly renewal of your visa is coming up in a few days and-"

"You wouldn't!" Arren gasped.

"It can get terribly sticky at foreign affairs, especially in unusual cases such as yours ..." she said, a threat lingering in her voice.

Arren clenched her teeth. "What you're asking is wrong. You want me to use my technology and that gives you an unfair advantage over other countries."

"And you don't think they're putting their alien guests to work as well?" she asked, sounding bothered.

Arren folded her arms and turned her head to face the wall. "Fine."

"Good," Elizabeth replied. "I look forward to your report this evening."

***

Arren and Chase went up in the ship after dinner and were out of the atmosphere in seconds. Dad didn't want to go, and Lucky was too busy trying to get to the next level in, what was it this time, Skyrim, or something? It took only a few moments to locate the wayward satellite and pull up beside it.

"Here," Arren said, "let me show you a trick. Let's pop down to somewhere I don't usually like to go – processing."

Chase walked with her down several of the mismatched corridors, past mismatched doors and more corridors, till they eventually came to a large area about half the size of the indoor garden. Rows and rows of mining machines, pipes, cranes and pullies lined the room, all neatly organised and put away. In the centre of the room was a thick, clear floor, as wide as a netball field. Arren walked straight out over it.

Chase couldn't help himself; he walked up and stretched each foot out hesitantly. It looked just like glass.

"What's it made of?" he asked.

"What?" Arren replied.

"The floor," he asked again, placing one foot on the solid surface.

"Oh, diamond[28]," she said.

It certainly seemed very strong.

And there, just beneath the diamond floor, was a floating satellite. It was about the size of a large rubbish bin, with two huge solar panels sticking out either side. On one end there was a big satellite dish pointing towards the earth. The satellite was covered with gold coloured foil which was badly torn down one side.

"Well," Arren announced in a voice like a repair man, "Thar's yer problem!"

"Are we going to fix it?" Chase asked.

Arren didn't look pleased. "Might as well. I just fear that once I've done one favour for them they'll expect the world."

She looked down at the little satellite, floating soundlessly in the vacuum of space, then sighed.

The next thing Chase knew, the little satellite started floating up through the floor.

Chase jumped back just in case the floor had disappeared, forgetting for a moment that Arren would never let that happen. It was just really interesting how she could make solid objects not interact with each other, like one of them wasn't even there.

It arrived on the diamond floor and sat there. Chase went up to take a good look at it. He poked at the golden foil.

"What's it made out of?" he asked.

"Gold," she replied.

---

[28] Actually, diamonds aren't rare, they're quite common. Only the diamonds that are gem stone quality are rare. Diamonds are made of carbon, which is as common as coal (coal is made of carbon too). Scientists learnt how to make artificial diamonds way back in around 1953, so it's not too hard to imagination an entire floor made of diamond if you had advanced technologies to help you!

"Gold!" he shouted. "How much do you reckon this thing is worth?"

"The entire satellite took four point eight million dollars to build[29]. But there's not actually that much gold there, less than fifty grams[30], not worth much more than two thousand dollars. Gold can stretch out really, really far."

"Why'd they use gold?" he asked.

"They - oh, you just love working on that science project don't you." she replied, getting enthusiastic.

"Whaaa?" he wondered what she was going on about.

"Gold foil protects the satellite from the radiant energy of the sun. It also helps to conduct the heat away from the heat sensitive parts of the satellite."

"Reckon gold would help our science project?" He rubbed his hands greedily, not really expecting gold foil to turn up.

"Sure, all we need is about two hundred Olympic sized swimming pools full of sea water to produce about a gram of gold[31]. There's lots of gold floating in the sea. But while gold has the highest capacity to conduct heat and electricity of any pure metal, aluminium foil is muuuuch cheaper."

"Can you collect gold from the ocean?" Chase asked.

"Yeah, it'd take a couple of hours to construct the mining gear on the ship, then we'd have about four grams a day. But I'm NOT going to do it!"

Somehow he knew she'd say that.

"Wait, so if we coat our box in some kind of reflective material it might keep out the heat?"

"Yes, but it will also keep the heat in."

"How do we get the heat out then? What absorbs heat?"

"Dark things, black paint, etc., to begin with at least."

---

[29] In 1998.
[30] This satellite uses 48.25 grams.
[31] It takes about a hundred million kilograms to produce 1 gram at 10 parts per trillion, check here.

"So, foil on the outside to keep the sunlight out, dark on the inside to keep it cool."

"Yeah, you should try that."

"Oh, I will, I will!" And he gave an evil laugh. It sure would be good to have a little gold for this science project, but it would be *nice* to have four grams of gold every day.

2 How to fix a satellite

"So," he said, coming out of his fantasy, "how do we fix it?"

"Oh, sorry. I was thinking about designing a machine to recycle the gold from the air in the factories that make computer parts. Here, fix it with this."

She held out her hand and a nearby cupboard flew open. A headband flew out of it and through the air to land in her outstretched hand.

"How do you keep doing that?" Chase asked, amazed.

"Inside this ship I have a lot of control over matter. Here's one way to explain how to make things fly around, and it relates to our theory of heat: Particles are always in motion, it's how heat transfers. Bouncy particles wobble around and whack into each other, this is experienced by us as heat[32], as I said before. Now imagine that all those little bouncing patterns all just happened to bounce in the same direction at the same time? Then the whole object would move, correct? Well that's how I do it."

"Is that for real?"

She just smiled and didn't answer[33]. Instead she just said, "Here, try on the psycho-enhancing headband. You used it to reshape the metal hull last time. Now I'll show you how to use it to make things move through the air as your imagination directs them to."

"Really?"

"Here's a scrap of paper. Picture all the little particles in this paper bouncing happily around. Pressed up right next to each other because they're a solid, and so stuck together that they don't usually bounce each other away into the air. Always moving, moving, moving."

"OK," Chase put on the headband. "Jiggling little particles. Oh, yeah, I am imagining them."

"Now make them all jiggle in the same direction."

---

[32] They not only bounce, they also wobble like jelly in all sorts of ways to express that quality we know as heat. So they can have a lot of heat energy without going anywhere.

[33] The motion of particles is used as an explanation for psychokinesis, however, science has yet to accept any general account of how psychokinesis works, if it does at all. So no, not real, as far as we can tell.

Chase stared intently at the paper. He imagined the little sea of jiggling particles, but was surprised that his imagination pictured them more like long chains than individual little orbs. Maybe he was seeing the fibres? Or maybe the DNA? Paper was made from trees, and trees were alive after all. He tried to get all that jiggling to go one way, but they only seemed to be jiggling more and more ...

Suddenly the piece of paper burst into flames.

"Ahh!" he yelled and stomped it out.

Arren was too busy laughing to help. The smoke wafted up through the air.

"Oh look, hot air rises in the ship too," he muttered.

"Not bad, my apprentice. Very quick. Usually it takes humans a few days, and the Coebri I trained were all little kids too. It's very cultural to find pyrokinesis easier than psychokinesis. Hah, you burnt it up!"

"I don't think it's funny," he said. He was worried about what else he might accidently set on fire.

"Don't worry, Chase, you're not going to set fire to anything you don't want to. It's like lighting a match, you have to put in *effort* to do it. Carrying around a match doesn't mean you're about to start a fire."

"Mmm, hope not. Actually, can I use this technique to cool things down too?" he asked.

"Sure can," she replied. "Among the Coebri, it's one of the most common methods."

"Must be pretty useful," he muttered.

"Sure is, but there are pretty easy ways to heat things up to; electricity, friction, exothermic chemical reactions[34],

---

[34] Just to explain, every chemical reaction either releases heat (exothermic) or absorbs it (endothermic). Some endothermic chemical reactions as so intense they can create ice, and the Australian army uses that to make ice cream while out on patrol. Some exothermic chemical reactions release so much heat that they make the air glow – i.e., fire.

concentrating the radiant energy of the sun. Just to name just a few."

Chase nodded.

Arren continued, "So here's the puzzle. The sun is hot, too hot for your technology. And you've *never* been able to get, like, a teaspoon of sun. So how do your scientists know what the sun is made out of?"

"I have no idea," Chase confessed.

"By its *colour*," she said with a grin, pointing to the pictures on her screens. "When things get hot, they glow. Did you know you can tell exactly what is in a fire by what colour it is? That's how you know what's in the sun even though your people have never been there. When atoms get hot enough to glow we can tell exactly what kind of atom they are by their colour. It's called spectroscopy[35] and it was developed by loads of scientists over many years."

"So hot things glow," Chase summarized.

"Yep," she replied. "Most things glow in colours your eyes cannot see. For example, when aluminium is hot enough to melt your finger if you touch it, it glows in a colour your eyes can't see called ultraviolet light. So you can get sunburnt, but you can't see the aluminium glowing! It's one of the dangers of working with aluminium. Each substance will glow in different colours depending on their temperature."

"So that's what makes light globes work," Chase said.

"Pretty much," she agreed.

---

[35] Spectroscopy has a long and complex history, but began around 1826 when John Herschel and William Talbot reported their discovery that, when heated, different substances produced different rainbows (called spectrum). Just noticing the colour of an object is a form of spectroscopy, as it helps you know what makes up the substance. Neon lights are a good example, each gas produces a particular colour. Another fun example involves flames tests, which you use to produce green fire.

"So what happens if things get, like, even hotter than that?" Chase queried.

"Well, when you make atoms around a million degrees hot they begin to fuse together in a nuclear fusion reaction, creating *new* atoms; that's how the sun gets its energy. And if you keep getting hotter and hotter, with more and more energy, stranger things happen: like fundamental forces blending together, new particles popping into existence, and more!"

"Wow, I'd love to see that," he admitted.

She waved her hand and panels like television screens floated from the wall. They began to glowing with images straight from her imagination. Bright lights and flashes, impossible colours swirled like she was trying to depict the inside of a nuclear explosion. It was amazing.

"So that's how new atoms are made, inside stars," Chase said.

"As far as your people know," she replied, always indicating that there was more to learn if he wanted to ask.

"Hey, Arren. I was just wondering, what happens to things when they get really, really cold."

"They freeze. You know how those particles are moving all the time? And as they get colder they slow down more and more. Eventually they all stick together and you call that a solid. But you know that, right? But, believe it or not, that's not the end of the story."

"There's more?" Chase asked.

"Yes, Bose-Einstein condensates and superfluids. Really weird stuff. In 1924, a young scientist named Bose came up with the crazy idea that if things got even colder than a solid, even *stranger* things could happen; almost as if the atoms would begin to blend into each other. Einstein supported and evolved the idea. Scientists finally made some of the stuff in 1995 and called it a superfluid, and it does some *weird* things. Like, it has zero friction, it can crawl up the sides of the container it is in; and if you shine a light on it, *snap*, it heats up enough to turn back into a solid! Weird."

"That is weird," he said, admiring her images. Some of them looked like they came right off the internet.

"You know how one way to describe heat is with moving particles? Well, there is a temperature, called absolute zero, where all motion stops. It's -273.15 degrees Celsius[36]. Yet try as you might, there is nothing you can do to arrive at absolute zero. You can get closer and closer, but never actually arrive. Nothing gets colder than absolute zero."

"That's cool."

"Absolutely cool." She smiled, surrounded with the beauty of her dancing images. Atoms too small to be seen were forged and reforged in exploding stars. Mysterious metals turned liquid and began to climb their way up the container they were in, and then do even stranger things. Chase knew it was a beauty only the imagination could conceive, because no eye could ever safely witness nature at these extremes.

Chase sighed, but there was work to be done. "I suppose we'd better be getting back to our chores."

"Yep," she sighed. "Fix'n the satellite!"

He didn't really want to. He was worried he'd rip all the foil off and do so much damage not even Arren could fix it. But he also liked the idea of learning how to fix things without touching them. So he looked down at the foil. He imagined it was like water, flowing together to form a still pond ...

And in less than a second he'd zipped the torn foil up like new. He ripped off the headband, just in case.

"Did you see that?" he boasted.

---

[36] Or -459.67° Fahrenheit. Really, really cold. Impossibly cold. Nothing we can currently do can actually get to this really, really cold temperature.

"Yeah, wow," she replied, seeming really impressed.

"Zip! Just like that! I think I got the hang of it from the last time I tried. Yeah, it's really easy. You just gotta pretend the metal is water, not stone. Yeah, I diiid it, I diiiid it!"

"OK, don't get carried away," she smiled.

"Let's keep practicing," he said, and briefly danced another victory dance.

It took him an hour, but eventually he got the paper to move just a little. He was much better at creating fire; he even got to the point where he could create a little fire just out of thin air. This was especially difficult because all the hot air kept rising up, the cooler air replacing it. Chase could see it all in his mind's eye; the hot air would rise up until it hit the ceiling, run along the roof, hit the wall, cool down and fall on the floor, then run along the floor until it flowed back up again to fill the space between his hands once more.

Little convection currents warming up the processing deck with a P14 weather satellite and a diamond floor full of stars.

Chapter 9
The Trojan

The satellite was fixed.

"I suppose," Chase suggested, "we can just phase through this floor too when we get home? Just turn up in the living room. You know, avoid the whole air lock thing."

"Yes, but we shouldn't."

"Why not?"

"Because everything about me is built on another world: my engines, my landing pads, my animals and insects. There are microscopic life forms in the air here that really shouldn't be introduced onto Earth."

"Oh, that makes sense. You don't want to, um, introduce any alien species."

"Yep, that's it."

"So that's why we always come and go through the airlock?"

"Whenever we can, it's the simplest way."

Then Chase had a random thought. "Arren, you don't seem to make friends with the girls in class. I mean, you talk to them and all but you don't seem to be letting any of them become your friends. Why is that?"

She was silent for a moment. "Western cultures, like Australian … credit a lot of intuition to their females. I'm so convinced that every other night one of them dreams about me being an alien, or a machine, or both. You can't see what I see. They already know, unconsciously. I just don't want to have to answer any questions I can't answer truthfully yet," she replied.

But Chase thought that was a bit silly. She seemed to be very worried about what humans were capable of, especially with things like intuition and untapped potential.

"You know," she explained, guessing his thoughts, "I never dream. I have no unconscious mind, at least not like you. I have no ancestral memory[37] and you don't even notice yours. Sometimes ... sometimes I wonder what it would be like to dream of events your great, great grandmother experienced. I think that would be nice. I think that would be nice to ... belong, like that." She sighed.

"Still wishing you were human?"

"Something like that. But then, that's why I built this body in the first place. I wanted to experience the universe. I let my dad, Lord Tzaarkh, convince me it was a good idea."

They were silent, until a thought popped into Chase's head and he said it out loud without thinking. "You know, I don't think you need to worry about the girls like that. They won't know you're not human and if they do unconsciously, I don't think they'll worry about it. I wouldn't."

She looked at him, thinking for a moment.

"You know, Chase, if you believe I've nothing to fear from female intuition then I'm going to believe you. I don't have intuition, just a million random probabilities that can simulate all possible outcomes of any scenario imaginable. Oh, but to simply know without knowing *why* you know! That would be *great*."

Chase smiled. "But sometimes intuition turns out to be wrong."

---

[37] Ancestral or racial memories are the thoughts, feelings and experiences passed down the generations without being taught. The theory of genetic memories suggests this is achieved as our DNA is somehow capable of 'remembering' our experiences and can pass them to our children. Again, it is very difficult, if not impossible, to test this idea with our current understanding in science, and thus racial memories are not considered part of mainstream science.

"Yeah, I can see how that can be a problem," she agreed. They chatted more about the girls in class while they went to the airlock.

***

The scientist watched as the space ship left and entered a low earth orbit, stayed there a few hours, and then simply appeared back down on the surface of the planet.

We need to be careful now, Obi-jo signed to her.

That was so obvious, the scientist didn't bother replying.

Almost a month went by while they carefully collected data. They watched the space ship day and night, but they didn't dare use any active scanners; even the rod was a terrible risk. Most of the time, the invisible space ship followed the alien girl around. It went to school with her. It went to the park with her. Even at night it hovered around the strange house with crystals in the doorways and statues on the unkempt lawn. Occasionally, but only occasionally, it left her.

"What are they doing?" the scientist wondered one day.

Maybe she's already been converted? Obi-jo suggested.

"I don't think so," the scientist disagreed with disdain. Biology and neurology were her speciality, and the scan of that girl had been pretty conclusive. Although she looked human on the outside, and probably looked human on an x-ray, and though she would probably even be able to pass the average blood test, she was well and truly, without doubt, a biomechanical humanoid of alien origin. Too much about her was alien; her biochemistry was a mystery to even Earth's most successful bio-neurologist: herself.

Suddenly Obi-jo gave a hoot and dragged at her cuff once more.

"What do you *want*?" she said, the frustration evident in her voice.

I found something here, Obi-jo signed. *It's an internet access point running incredibly fast. I've never encountered anything like it. It is searching for information and wiping out any evidence of its path as it goes. It's amazing!*

"And?" she asked.

And it could be them! The orangutan signed. *It'd have to be. I've seen what they can do at the spy research division and this is nothing like that. It's different, almost … alien.*

Now the scientist was interested. She raced across to the ape's screen, filled with data and complex computer symbols.

The scientist was clever, very clever, but hexadecimal code was not her strong point, and it was the only language Obi-jo would program in. It was fortunate that Obi-jo excelled so much at computer programming; it was how she earned her keep.

And the little ape was earning it again today.

"Where?" the scientist insisted. "I don't see it!"

Obi-jo pointed to the screen in several places, signing something incomprehensible, then started typing on her hexadecimal keyboard again, battering it in a frantic rhythm.

"Quick! Find out where it came from. Trace it to its source."

Obi-jo screeched in frustration, and kept on typing madly. The scientist stepped back. Obi-jo probably was trying to do just that but lacked two extra hands to tell her. Still, surely there was something she could do about *that* one day.

Suddenly Obi-jo stopped.

"What is it?" she asked.

No firewall. Obi-jo replied.

"What, no … don't they expect to get hacked?"

Either they're from a place that doesn't steal, or they want us to get in, Obi-jo said. *I mean, they were hidden. But once you find the door there aren't any locks.*

"Be **careful**!" the scientist said in desperation, clutching Obi-jo's orange fur. But she knew she'd never have the physical strength to budge her.

Don't worry, we've got them now, Obi-jo explained. *I'm going to insert a host of bots – complex programs that will try to download as much of the hard drive as possible.*

"They'll notice that straight away," the scientist complained.

Yes, but it'll give us some info, maybe something useful. Besides, first I'm going to put in something that will let us keep a watch on them no matter what they do about the bots.

"What on earth would do that?" the scientist asked in disbelief.

A Trojan[38], Obi replied.

And the scientist smiled.

***

Arren squealed.

Then she sneezed.

"You alright?" the teacher asked her.

They were in maths class, about a month after the last market and less than a week till the second, and everyone was sitting there typing when Arren suddenly squealed.

"Is it a cockroach?" some girl asked, panic rising in her voice. "I bet it's a cockroach!"

---

[38] A Trojan is a computer program that looks harmless or even helpful, but once it gets into your computer, it can do mean things such as track the changes you make to your passwords or guide other computer viruses to your computer. In short, they are nasty. They are named after the famous Trojan horse, but that is another story and you shall be told ... another time.

Students near Arren began moving their chairs and looking around their feet.

But Chase was looking at Arren. He'd never seen that look on her face before, she was angry. He wasn't close enough to see, she was sitting with the girls in an attempt to socialise herself into their community, but he was sure her irises were flickering furiously.

"Arren?" the teacher asked.

"Whoa, she looks-" a student began.

"Treacherous thieves!" she suddenly stood up and shouted, "Cantankerous criminals!"

Everyone leaned well away from her. She started pacing back and forth, fists clenched.

"How could they? Chase! They ... how could they?" she demanded to know.

They all looked at him.

If only he knew what *she* was thinking.

"We're in maths class, Arren," he replied.

She looked around.

"What's she skitzing out for?" Mark T said with disgust.

Arren looked at him, harrumphed with exasperation and walked over to Chase.

"Sorry, you gotta sort this out *right now*," she said to him. She grabbed his hand and pulled him to his feet.

"We ... I ..." he tried to argue. But Arren was incredibly strong when she wanted to be.

"Wait a minute!" the teacher said. "You need a permission slip to leave class, young lady."

But by the time he'd grabbed one and scratched his signature on it, apparently OK with one student leaving with a crazed out girl, they'd already left.

As soon as they reached the hall Arren stopped walking. The teacher walked out and, to Chase's amazement, walked right through him, looking around as if he couldn't see them at all. Then the walls flowed downwards as if he was floating up through the roof.

"What? How?" Chase asked.

"We're in *me*, you know, my ship, Chase."

"You keep it at the school now?"

"I keep it wherever I go," she said, still sounding annoyed.

"What, even at night? I thought you kept it at Ms Garibaldi's place?"

She looked sad.

"Would you prefer I did that?" she whispered.

"No, I mean, maybe?" he stumbled. "Look, tell me what's going on."

"I'll show you," she said.

They were in the airlock; Chase could see now that the regular ship was visible around them, now that he'd been shifted into the same dimension. He had to assume it was there all the way through maths class and Arren had taken him over to the other side as soon as they'd entered the hall, making it look like they were walking out when in fact they were stepping into another dimension. They ran to the control room.

Then the ship teleported, disappearing from the school and appearing right above some modern looking office buildings that were surrounded by parks. There was some curious looking industrial equipment nearby, so it might have been a research facility of some kind.

"Oh! Look how upset I am," Arren complained. "I missed it by three nanometres!"

"What do you mean?" Chase asked as they floated towards the nearest building.

"I just did a little teleport across your city. No wormholes, just good old fashion tunnelling. And I missed! You know what the only computer capable of flawlessly tunnelling across the entire universe of space is?" she asked.

"Umm."

"The human soul," she concluded[39], and began floating through the walls of the office building. People were walking around, doing their own thing, not seeing them. Chase still winced every time they floated through a wall in case it hit him, but he knew that was impossible unless Arren placed them back into their regular dimension instead of the one her ship was now in.

Arren slowed down when she reached her destination, and Chase gasped. There, sitting at the head of a table full of a dozen suited and important looking people, was his mother.

She was saying something about finances when Arren interrupted. Chase could see everyone like they were all in the same dimension, even though he knew he and Arren weren't. It was as if she was allowing the light to interact with her so they could see her, but she would still be as insubstantial as a ghost to them.

"What do you think you're *doing*?" Arren demanded, stepping back into normal reality.

People at the table gasped, and two of them screamed. Costa whipped out his gun so fast Chase didn't see him do it. In the next instant, Costa fitted the glowing green and ethereal attachments to it and from his dimension, Chase could see it had four weird wafting tentacles attached to it. It looked even more dangerous in this place than in the normal world.

"What are you doing here?" he shouted.

"Why didn't the alarms work?" another protested.

---

[39] Sci-fi. But wouldn't it be cool if it turns out one day that we don't need anything to travel across space and the stars: our minds and bodies can already do it if we *believe* enough. No spaceships or anything!

"Shut up!" Arren demanded.

"Enough," Chase heard his mum say, and people stopped speaking. "Child, why have you interrupted this meeting? You know it is breach of your visa to interfere with the Australian Government in any way."

"Oh, so it's OK for you to do it to me, but when I pop in unannounced it's all 'off limits'," she said harshly.

Mum did not look impressed. "What are you talking about?"

"You know very well what I'm talking about!" Arren shouted.

Chase looked around the room. Somehow he could tell his Mum didn't know what Arren was talking about. No-one knew what she was talking about. Not even he knew why Arren was transporting him into his mum's meeting.

"I don't think they do," he told her.

Arren paused then spoke directly into his mind. *Really? Well, keep quiet anyway, they might sense you and I don't want them to realise you're here yet.*

He'd assumed that.

Arren calmed down and took a breath. "One point three minutes ago someone accessed my central processing system and released a series of self-replicating computer programs, that downloaded one trillionth of one per cent of my data. They *stole* it. I want to know who did it and I want that data back," she shouted.

Mum looked concerned.

"I have no information about this attack," she replied, "and unless we have a rogue element somewhere in this room I do not know anyone who could have performed this operation."

Arren folded her arms in disbelief.

"Why was your data so easy to hack?" Costa asked like this was all Arren's fault.

She stumbled over her words. "It's not. It's not easy, I mean, you had to be looking for me to find it. So it had to be one of *you*."

"I doubt any of us would jeopardise our employment or personal safety by hacking into an alien life form." Mum argued. "But it does beg the question about the ease of access. Have you no security? No passwords, no firewall? Surely you would be aware if someone was trying to gain access."

Arren said nothing for a moment. "No. I ... once they're in I can't tell if it's someone else or just a random thought of my own."

"You're risking your entire knowledge base on the vain hope that the people of this planet will be disinclined to hack into your computer systems?" Mum asked in exasperation.

"OK. OK!" Arren conceded. "I'll ... upgrade myself. I'll give myself three levels of multifractional mutating analogues. Stuff you Earthlings haven't even heard of yet. But I want to know who took my data and why!"

"So do we ... " Costa said, holding his gun dangerously.

"And you can't have it. I want it back."

"Do you know what they took?" Mum asked.

"Loads of random stuff: Pictures from my childhood, conversations I've heard. It's hard to tell, I couldn't track the programs. It's so unfair; you see, where I come from we don't steal from each other. No-one ever stole from me," she said, almost seeming sad that she was so poor that she never had anything worth stealing.

"I will order a full inquiry into this, immediately. Charles, will you be able to get what details we have of the hacking from our young visitor here?"

"Done," Arren said. "I just sent them to his tablet."

"You just hacked his tablet?" Costa accused her.

"There isn't a door on this planet I can't open," she boasted, "or a computer I can't hack. The only reason I don't do it is because I don't have permission. Ms Elizabeth gave me *permission* Costa. And I'd thank all you Earthlings to respect my privacy just as I respect yours."

Chase thought she made it sound like it was their fault. Then he realised that maybe she *was* speaking to all humanity, telling them so that it would filter through the group subconscious or something.

"Very well," Chase's mother said in her professional way. "Please leave us, we have important matters to discuss-"

"Wait," Chase cut her off. She stopped mid-sentence, even though there was no way she could have heard his voice.

He walked up to her. Everyone in the room was silent. Costa began to reach for some sunglasses.

Chase, Arren muttered to his mind.

"Put me in there," he begged. "I need to ... talk to Mum."

She nodded.

The room gasped again as Chase appeared. Costa almost pointed his gun at him, but held it down at the last instant.

Chase looked at his mum, right within arm's reach.

"Hello, young man," she said.

Her voice was polite, but it was cold, like all the feeling had died from it a long time ago.

"Elizabeth," Chase stated.

For a moment, just a brief moment, some feeling flittered past her porcelain façade. It was like all the feelings in the world were in there, trapped away in some impossible-to-open bottle.

He held out his hand to shake hers and after a moment she took it, everyone standing by wearily. Chase could feel it in her hands too; they were cold, like the feelings were all asleep. She wasn't angry, or sad. She was just ... asleep.

"What happened?" he asked her. He wanted to know why she'd disappeared when they were four, leaving his dad heartbroken, leaving their house and lives a mess.

For a moment she didn't say anything.

"Has your father told you nothing?" she replied.

He shrugged.

"I suggest you take it up with him," she said in a tone that was dismissive. Chase could tell it wasn't supposed to be insulting, she was just being matter-of-fact.

But he didn't have a clue how to talk to his dad about … that kind of thing.

He was sad, and let it show. He turned to leave when suddenly there was a whirlwind of feelings from his mother. He didn't even stop to ask how he knew; he just turned, expecting to see her bursting into tears. Instead it was the same cold face, the same emotionless smile.

"Do … take care, young one," she said.

She couldn't even call him 'son'.

But he didn't complain. He just nodded, then turned and he and Arren shifted out.

Chapter 10
The second market

The day of the second market had arrived.

"It happens *today*," the scientist declared, tying her hair up once more, putting on her washed jacket. It was time for the direct approach. That, or time for something desperate. "I'm tired of sneaking around. It happens *today*."

Obi-jo did not reply. She was busy studying the massive complication of data and images from the alien and her spaceship. Most of it was useless, but they'd learnt a lot in the short time since the Trojan had been placed. A lot, such as all her new passwords, all her new access codes, all her command files.

"It is time," the scientist repeated, trying to steer the ape away from her screen. She would never admit it, but she needed her support before beginning something that had to be seen through to the end. Something that could be so dangerous.

But we're not ready, wait! Obi-jo insisted.

"Wait? I've done my waiting! For *ten years* I've waited. It happens *today*!"

The orangutan watched her in silence as images from the alien girl's memories flickered across the screen. Images of a little girl holding a strange man's hand, a man who had one glowing red eye. She looked happy.

"But there is work to be done." Without regret, the scientist reached over and switched the memory off with disgust.

***

Chase felt sick. The second market was an even bigger success, and everyone was very excited. The school had already purchased a new netball set with the sudden influx of cash, and every single recess and lunch people were using it. Everyone wanted to see what they'd buy from the second market.

At first, Chase couldn't be more excited too.

But by mid-morning Chase wasn't feeling so excited anymore; he was feeling ill. Someone was giving away homemade marshmallows and they weren't very good, but he liked them. Somehow the word had gotten around that Chase would eat them, so over the course of the day over a hundred marshmallows were being politely handed over to him so that the poor soul making them never knew how unpopular they really were.

Now he was in real danger of vomiting them all back up.

So how Arren had convinced him to try out her new ride he'd never know. She had built a hovercraft.

A yellow, three person, real life hovercraft.

It roared like thunder; everyone could hear it and kids had been lining up all day to take a ride with her. She laughed again as she brought it to rest, and the excited kids and grownups jumped out.

"Hey, Chase, take a ride with me!"

It was hard to say no to her, so in spite of feeling like barfing up marshmellowy chunks all over the shiny new covering, he was sitting in the hovercraft.

"Your people should really invest some more research into the potential of hovercrafts," she said, checking her dials and waiting for people to stand back far enough to start again. "Really, they only use one tenth the amount of energy a car does."

"Well, they're making energy efficient cars now," Chase retorted, clutching the side of the craft, knowing this ride was a bad idea.

3 A real live hovercraft

"And thank goodness for that! But even so cars have a weakness that they can never overcome – wheels. At least one tenth of *their* energy just goes into overcoming the wheels' resistance to turning, I mean, the friction in the wheels as they rub along the axle[40]. With a hovercraft almost all the energy goes into motion. They are just really, really energy efficient. And they don't need tyres. Do you

---

[40] Not friction against the road, that is a good thing. Without friction between the road and tyres, cars would not only never stop, they would spin their wheels in a useless spinout instead of going anywhere.

know how much waste tyres make in the world every day[41]? Terrible!"

"OK, I promise to look into it just after, whoa!" he said as she took off, laughing. He wondered why she never seemed to get bored of taking new passengers along for the same ride again and again. Chase clutched the edge of his seat, trying to stop the nausea in his stomach as they took another steep corner. He felt his stomach lurch.

Arren suddenly slowed down at looked at him in concern. "Had enough?"

He nodded.

"You should try jellybeans. I like jellybeans."

"I'll have to remember that," Chase said as his stomach gave another involuntary lurch.

She smiled again, and slowly returned to the launch bay. When they got there a large man with a red beard was waiting for them.

"Hey," he said, "that's one great hovercraft."

"Thanks," Arren said.

"Mind if I take it for a spin?"

"Sure, let me show you how."

"My name's Marton," he said.

"And they call me Arren," she replied with a big smile.

Chase stumbled from the passenger seat and rested against the barrier, his green face and obvious nausea in no way discouraging the eager man. Dozens of kids were pressing their noses to the fence or getting told off for

---

[41] Over 1 billion tyres are made in the world each year. In 2010, around 20 million tyres were thrown out in Australia alone (almost one per person in the country)! Where do old tyres go? Most become landfill waste. Tyres aren't biodegradable, but they can be recycled. The good news is that there are lots of things old tyres can become, including roads, playground turf and equipment, lightweight construction material, and even fuel. Worldwide waste tyre production is a problem but like most problems, it can be also be an opportunity.

sitting on the hay bales that protected them from the thundering craft.

"Hey," Lucky said walking up, "you having fun?"

Chase glared at his brother. No, he was *not* having fun, and thought it was so *obvious* that he didn't want to reply. That, and he really did think saying anything right now might make him coat the hay bales with a thin, sugary coating of puke.

"Gee, those kids sure like the hovercraft," Lucky said, smiling as he changed the topic. "How much have you made?"

"About two hundred dollars, I think," Chase replied, trying to take deep breaths. "She charges a dollar a minute, and most people take a two minute ride. She's been at it all morning."

"Still, I think that guy likes it most of all," Lucky observed. And indeed he did. They had landed and he was having a conversation with Arren, checking over the hovercraft and looking at it from underneath. Arren called them over.

"What is it?" Chase asked.

"He wants to know where your dad got the designs for the hovercraft," she replied.

"Off the internet, I guess," Chase stated. Well, OK, that wasn't *really* honest since Arren had designed it all herself: from scratch.

"Look, that's inert gas welding," Marton stated with excitement. "Quality work! I'm impressed."

"Arren helped him make it," Chase said, trying to make up for lying.

Marton walked around the hovercraft once or twice more.

"I'll take it," he stated with a grin.

"Yippee," Arren shouted, "Now Ms Garibaldi can finally go to Italy!" she said.

"How much did you just sell it for?" Chase asked.

"Ten thousand dollars."

"Ten thousand …" Chase felt dizzy again.

"That much?" Lucky agreed.

Marton answered, "You're joking, that's a *steal!* Just look at this sideboard, thick plastic, not that cheap moulding. And this reconditioned motor looks like it's been made up better than new! I've *always* wanted a hovercraft! Give me a chance to get around the farm without breaking up my soil. Really excited about that."

"You should be," Arren said, "but you'll have to wait till tonight, there are still some kids who still need rides."

"Kids," he said with disgust, looking eager to get his hands on his new toy, or was it his 'professional farming equipment'. "Well, all right."

"Looks like the big kids don't want to wait for the little kids before they get their hands on their new toy," Lucky whispered.

Dad came running over; Arren sent him texts every time she wanted to speak to him. He was only too happy to take farmer Marton's cheque, only just hiding his surprise at all the zeros on it. Even though he'd known that she was making a hovercraft from all the junk lying around Ms Garibaldi's yard and even though she'd told him how much it was worth and all about the construction process so that he could answer most intelligent questions about how it was made. Lucky had told everyone that his Dad was making a hovercraft with Arren's help, but anyone who dug in with a few questions usually seemed to get the impression that Arren had made a hovercraft with Dad's help. Such questions might have led them to question how such a young person might manage inert gas welding, people with questions like Marton.

Thankfully, in the end, Marton didn't seem to care where the hovercraft came from at all. It was neat, slimline, strong and sounded like thunder. And that, it seemed in farmer Marton's books, was just what was needed.

And then Mum turned up.

Lucky gasped and pointed.

Chase turned and saw her black car parking out the front of the principal's office, right inside the disabled parking section like she didn't even care. Two men with dark sunglasses and suits got out; one of them looked like Flannigan. They got out of the car and stood still, looking unfriendly.

She swept into the market grounds, dressed in a professional business skirt and blouse, and wearing the same dark sunglasses as last time. She stuck out among the happy people like a black dog at a party for white cats. In short, Chase realised, she was dressed to dominate, not to connect.

She approached the hovercraft ride. She looked right at Arren, not even acknowledging anyone else.

Arren made her wait, making sure all the kids were safe while the sports teacher took a few of them for rides. Then Arren walked over to talk to her. Chase would have joined them, but Arren seemed to read his thoughts and shook her head at him.

Chase was too far away to hear what was said but they seemed to be whispering anyway. Chase could hear nothing until he heard Arren say, 'No'. Then she said it again, and again, whipping her hands in front of her in a dismissive gesture. Shaking her head furiously, she walked off.

"Arren!" Mum shouted at her.

Arren walked over and stood next to Lucky and Chase.

Mum seemed angry but it was hard to tell with the sunglasses on. Then she turned to leave without saying another word.

"Hey, Mum," Lucky said as if he didn't have a care in the world.

She turned and stalked up to them and spoke before Lucky got to say anything. "Your misplaced concern for neutrality puts our entire civilisation in jeopardy, Arren. Your hosts, your friends, my sons. Please reconsider your decision in this matter."

She said it with such passion, like the whole country was at stake. But it was so weird, Chase felt nothing. Like she was just using words but didn't *feel* anything. He watched her sadly as the black car drove away.

"What's that about?" Lucky asked Arren, a slight frown on his face.

"I can never tell you," Arren replied.

"Nice of her to go speaking about her sons," Dad muttered, "without even saying their names."

Chase looked at the empty car park. His mother was right, it was time for answers, and those answers had to come from Dad.

Suddenly a crackling bolt of electricity lit up the blue sky. Arren yelped and, clutching her stomach, fell to the floor. Chase knelt down next to her as he watched the lightning fork and twist in the sky, following a strange pattern. He took a moment to recognise it – it was following the outline of one corner of Arren's ship. An instant later, the edge of the ship partially materialised into the normal dimension. It was very difficult to see it as it blended in with the bright blue sky, but it would still be a very weird sight even if you didn't know what to look for.

An instant later the ship rocketed upwards, off into space, trailing lightning. A sudden breeze struck the fairgrounds, distracting everybody once again. Most people laughed, thinking how strange it was, not knowing what had really happened.

What has just happened? Chase wondered. He turned to talk to Arren.

She answered his silent questions without being asked. "I don't believe it. That was singularly the most stupid thing I've ever witnessed."

He waited.

"Someone," Arren replied, "just hit me with a transdimensional gravitic anchoring device[42]. They tried to force me, the entire ship, right into normal space. It *could* have killed everyone here. I don't believe it."

"Who would want to do something like that?" Chase wondered, a little worried that Arren's spaceship was somewhere that it could have accidentally done some real harm, even if it was someone else's fault. "You don't suppose it was the Coebri?"

"No, they'd never risk killing someone without a fight, and I don't think it was the Federal Police, or your mum. They like keeping me a secret. No, it was someone who was trying to reveal me, show everyone the ship. Someone smart enough, or with the right kind of friends, to get their hands on a transdimensional gravitic anchoring device. But they'd still have to be ignorant enough to realise it might have killed people ... I can't think of anyone like that."

Chase pondered for a moment. "Where is the device now?"

"Stuck in the ship, the spiders are dissecting it now. It looks like it was buried in the ground a few weeks ago, I don't have any video footage of who might have buried it ... this is a bit concerning, I wonder who's looking for me?"

"The same person who pinged you last time?"

"No, impossible. A ping I can believe, but an anchoring device? That's not human technology. I'm guessing it was left there by accident, I don't know anyone foolish enough to try and forcibly materialise an entire spaceship right on

---

[42] Sci-fi: A device for forcing shifted objects into other dimensions.

top of a school fair. That was excessively ludicrous; the explosion could have levelled the town!"

She didn't seem so bothered now and stood up smiling. But Chase *was* worried. And it was there again ... that feeling ... like they weren't really safe right now ...

***

The scientist flung herself into her modified Volkswagen. *That was close, too close.* It was obvious now that she'd pushed things too far and that the little alien girl would be hunting around for answers now. Perhaps Obi-jo was right; it was time to wait just a little bit more.

Then she smiled. Now the alien would be vulnerable. Now the ship would have to leave its constant vigil over that messy house to answer questions. That would be the time, the time to strike.

Cold laughter echoed from the old orange van and Obi-jo, if there had been room, would have edged just a little further away.

Chapter 11
Mum

That evening Chase decided it was finally time for some answers. He found Dad in the backyard pottering around. He was pulling weeds from around Lucky's new vegetables which were growing really well. He was also half-heartedly weeding some of his old pot plants, most of which were no longer alive, surrounded by misplaced bricks that hadn't been moved in over eight years.

Arren followed Chase out and Lucky tagged along behind them just to see what was happening.

"Dad," Chase just came right out and asked him. "What happened with you and Mum?"

Dad scratched his chin and turned to scuff out some weeds with his boot. He took a really big breath and sighed. "I promised myself I wouldn't tell you till you were ready, and that you weren't ready until you asked. But now ... seems I don't really know what to say," he said it like it was an apology. "Where do you want me to start?"

Chase shrugged. "Just start from the beginning, Dad."

"OK, OK," he said, and sat down on a large cement planter box. "From the beginning ... you know the first time I saw your mother was at university. I was picking up an extra subject in my final year, and she was overloading her subject choices in her first. History and Philosophy of Science, I think it was. First time I ever laid eyes on her I remember thinking, 'Oh, now there's a girl I need to meet' ... but when I heard her speak for the first time, wow! I couldn't think of anything else for days. She was clearly a genius: witty, committed, intelligent. And she just loved to challenge the lecturer, make him think, force him to justify every claim he made. It was classic, beautiful."

"So she was a trouble maker as well?" Lucky asked.

"Big time, but I don't think she ever meant it. She just wanted to be precise, wanted to get it right. Knew not to trust lecturers *all* the time – especially those that acted like they never got it wrong and had nothing to learn. I was in a band at the time, and we used to play to the student union. She'd come by to listen. Never spoke to anyone, just sat there reading while everyone else socialised. It was weeks before I got the courage to speak to her, but soon as I did it, it turns out she was, well, she liked me too. We got talking and then, I guess, we fell in love."

"Aww, how nice," Arren said.

"Yeah, she was unlike anyone I'd ever met. Clever, gentle ... she used to sing. We used to do that every Friday, she'd sing along while I played guitar."

"You play guitar?" Lucky said, his arms folded in disbelief.

"Used to."

"So you fell in love, then we came along," Chase continued the story.

"Not quite, you boys came along two years later. We were already engaged. You know, now I look back on things it was pretty clear that she was working for the Feds, or secret service, or something already. She was just too darn clever. And me, I never wanted any part of that world. So she kept it all from me. Never really told me what she did for work and I never asked."

He paused before continuing, "But then when you boys arrived on the scene she just dropped it all. Said she was leaving work and becoming a full time mum. But I guess it was a tougher job than she realised. Something happened four months after you were born – now I don't want you to go blaming yourselves, but my dad took a fall and broke his leg and I had to go out to the hospital. By the time I got back to your mum she was, please try to understand, she was sitting at the kitchen table reading a book while you two screamed your lungs out. It was like she'd entirely forgotten you were there. That was my first real indication that she wasn't handling the change into full time motherhood so well."

"Postnatal depression?" Arren asked.

Dad shrugged, and nodded. "I had no idea she was suffering so much. She kept her world all so tightly together that I didn't even notice she was falling apart. Yet even then she refused to get help, she just dumped all the parenting on me from that day on. Not that I mind, being a dad is the best thing that's ever happened to me. But she changed from that day. She stopped smiling, stopped singing. She got right back into her career the next week. She was gone more and more. I tried to talk to her, tried to tell her to get some help. But she wouldn't. She just had to handle it all on her own. She got sick, and wouldn't let anyone help."

"Postnatal depression[43] isn't a weakness," Arren said, "it's an illness, and one that can be treated."

"I know," Dad said helplessly. "There was a time there, when you boys were about three, that I thought I might have been getting through to her. But then she just snapped right back and was worse than ever before. She never said goodbye. Just kept drifting further and further away until one day I realised she was not coming home. Got herself a

---

[43] Postnatal depression is a serious mental condition affecting around 15% of all mothers, which can be a difficult situation for the entire family. It is normal to feel stress over the big change of having a baby in one's life, but it's important to know the difference between postnatal depression and the fact that becoming a parent is usually a difficult experience. New (and experienced) parents need all the help they can get, and thankfully there's plenty out there for those who ask.

place in the city closer to her work. Never even thought of inviting us. Just got too busy …"

He sighed. It was a story that had been waiting a long time to be told.

"That kind of stuff hurts," Dad muttered in a soft voice, like a river that had flowed over rocks and rapids for many miles until it finally rested in a quiet sea.

It's not very easy to watch your Dad tear up but Chase didn't turn away. Chase was tearing up too.

Then Lucky laughed.

"Look at you two sob babies." Lucky smiled, but Chase could see the water rimming his eyes as well.

"I never heard that before," Chase said.

"I made myself promise that I'd never tell you 'till you asked," Dad repeated.

"What?" Chase choked, a little frustrated. "But that left me thinking you never wanted to talk about it at all!"

"Really?" Dad said. Clearly he'd never realised this before.

They just looked at each other, Chase wondered what to say.

"Postnatal depression is a form of mental illness," Arren repeated, sounding like she was trying to be helpful, "with measurable biochemical and neurological changes. The nervous system begins to shut down. It can make parents feel tired and hopeless, so the longer they put it off, the harder it becomes for them to make the decision to get help. But when they do go to their doctor, they find out that many others have faced the same thing, and there are many willing to help them to get better."

"Sounds like Mum wasn't cut out to be a, well, mum." Lucky said.

"Not at all, Lucky!' Arren replied, 'Behavioural and cultural expectations are closely tied –".

"Dad, Mum tried to do it all on her own, didn't she?" Chase interrupted the lecture.

Dad thought for a moment. "Parenthood is tough, everyone needs help. But I guess she just thought herself too tough to ask for help."

"Really?" Lucky wondered.

"Hard to say," Dad said, "but she loves you boys, I know."

Chase wanted to find out if his Dad had really done everything he could to help. He wanted to know if his mum really had been too stressed to care anymore. It didn't seem natural to abandon your kids for work. Yet even if he didn't understand it, it was what had happened to him, and he would have to find a way to live with that.

"There is a way to find out if she is still suffering depression, and working on treating it," Arren said.

"Go on," Chase urged.

"We need to get a blood scan."

"Blood scan on Mum?" he asked.

"Yes, it would be better to get a sample but you're not allowed to do that without her permission in your country. Unless she's incapable of deciding and you have enduring power of attorney?[44]" she asked Dad.

"Enduring, what now?" he asked, popping his head up.

"Thought not," she said like she half expected it. "Well, I guess I'll just have to make a compassionate call. Chase, Lucky, Dad, do I have your permission to get a blood and cerebral scan of your wife and mother?"

"Yep!" Chase agreed without pause.

"I'm not sure," Dad said, "as long as you don't hurt her in any way."

---

[44] <u>Enduring power of attorney</u> is the legal right in Australia to make important personal or financial decisions on behalf of someone else who might not be able to due to disability or ill health.

"Actually, with the technology I'm going to use it will do her only good. But I'll still need permission and if I can't get hers, I'll need yours."

"Well, you got it," he answered.

Lucky harrumphed as he flung himself on the outdoor arm chair that had been lying out there for years.

"Lucky?" she asked.

"Do you *need* my permission?" he said in a grumpy voice.

"No."

He paused. "Whatever."

"It's for her good!" Chase argued.

"I said *whatever!*" he grumped. "Go ahead, not that you *need* permission, they scanned *me* all over."

"You don't want to come this time, either," Chase guessed.

Lucky winked and pointed at Chase, meaning *got it in one.*

Dad sighed, patted him on the knee, and got up to make dinner.

Arren got to work on the machine right away. It took the whole evening to build it inside her spaceship. Actually, as Lucky noted, that was probably a worry. If she could build a super advanced alien scanning device in one evening why did it take her a whole month to build a hovercraft? Why did Arren insist on doing things the old fashioned way *outside* her ship?

In the end, Chase thought, *it doesn't matter. It is how we'll get some answers tonight.*

About midnight they left, appearing outside a large apartment building. It took Chase only a moment to realise it was in walking distance of where his mum worked. In the driveway there was a sleek black car, like the one she used to visit them in, parked next to a dusty orange Volkswagen. The contrast was distracting.

They floated through the walls of her apartment. The apartment was large, large enough for a whole family but it was sparse, as if she only ever used a few rooms. And it was neat. *Painfully* neat. Even the dust looked organised.

Mum was lying in the bed on her back, completely still. It reminded him uncomfortably of an Egyptian mummy. On her bedside table, in open view, was a well-used Enya CD, a glass of water and a bottle of pills.

"Medicine?" Chase asked Arren.

She smiled. "Antidepressants. Maybe she is more aware of her condition than we realised."

Carefully, from their own dimension, Arren's scanning machine floated into place. It looked like a strange, silver, crescent moon, covered in faint glowing lights. The scan only took an instant and Arren wouldn't let Chase speak.

Suddenly Mum sighed. Chase almost shouted out with fright. Then she muttered something that sounded like, "Such a good girl," and went right on sleeping.

Carefully they floated out the walls. Chase gave an enormous sigh of relief and opened his mouth to ask Arren when the scans would be complete.

"Ethylmetholtrethadine," she suddenly said.

"Ethyl ... metal ... wha?" Chase asked, briefly wondering if it might be a friend of hers.

"It's a psychotropic[45] medicine; I didn't think your people had invented it yet[46]. It can increase intelligence and concentration, but in the kinds of doses I'm finding here it creates a kind of devotion to cause and unyielding focus that is, well, unhealthy. It's has been added to her regular dosage of antidepressant pills. I think someone is messing with your mother's medicine!"

---

[45] Means 'affecting the mind'.
[46] They haven't. I made this up.

Chase was silent as a million feelings all exploded inside him at once, and for a moment he didn't know what to think. At first he was desperately relieved. He *knew* there was something wrong with Mum, and he *knew* it wasn't all her fault. Yet at the same time he felt unimaginably, irrationally angry at whoever was doing this to her. He quickly dismissed the thought that she might be doing it to herself.

"Also," Arren continued, "she had a spatial distortion alarm; they knew I might pay a visit. I think I managed to trick it so that no-one will know we were there." Arren said, then looked at him with concern. "Your blood pressure is way up."

"I …" he began, "We've *got* to tell her."

"I agree, but then she'll know we scanned her."

"Can't you just find out about the Ethyl stuff some other way? Some way that's not unusual."

"I suppose we can just *smell* her. Most psychotropic drugs change a person's natural scent but humans don't usually notice, at least on a conscious level[47]. It is possible though. Yes, now I know what to look for I can use a smell to infer that she's under the effects of Ethylmetholtrethadine, but it's still going to be difficult to establish without her baseline data."

"It's worth a try. You are, after all, a super advanced alien. They're going to believe whatever you say!" he said.

"I only wish that were true," she replied.

"We *have* to tell her," Chase repeated, more to himself.

"OK, we'll tell her next time we see her. Come on, let's take the scenic route back home."

"I *knew* it," Chase repeated.

---

[47] Some dogs, for instance, have been trained to detect cancer in urine samples. One Labrador, Daisy, has at least a 76% accuracy. This dog even found an early cancer in the woman who was training her to detect cancer by smell!

Chapter 12
Visit from a scientist

Lucky jumped as he heard a sudden knock at the door.

He was sitting on the lounge room floor playing 'Call of Duty' with unbroken intensity. Whatever Arren had done to him had increased his mental concentration immensely. He knew where his whole team were just by listening through the headset. He memorised every map they went through, instantly. He never felt nervous when they pulled into unfamiliar terrain.

He had to thank her for that, but he hadn't told her. He hadn't told anyone yet.

But he ignored the visitor. He was listening so hard to the game that he didn't hear the visitor's first few questions. He didn't hear the tension in his Dad's voice grow. He didn't hear his Dad telling the visitor to go away.

But he did hear the sudden explosion, a pulse of air that knocked the headset off his head. He heard his Dad being thrown against the entry cupboard, smacking his head and falling to the floor.

Lucky jumped to his feet in one move.

He turned around to see a short woman with dark hair who looked very much like his mother, only her hair was unkempt and tumbling over her shoulders from under a strange looking stack hat coated in foil.

"What are you doing here?" he warned her.

"Where is the alien?" she replied, pointing a dangerous looking device, like a mini double barrelled wrist gun, at him. The device she'd no doubt used on dad who was lying against the broken cupboard door, the mess spilling out over him. Lucky hoped he was allright, but somehow knew he'd be OK.

"I don't know what you mean," Lucky lied.

"I've been staking out this house for more than a month, boy. It lives here. I know it's here!"

"You're nuts! What did you do to my dad?"

She looked over and smiled. Then she looked back and Lucky realised he'd just missed his chance to make a move. He was fast, he'd have had her in just a –

"He'll be fine," she replied, as if she was trying to convince herself. "The SRAD[48] Mini emits a percussive blast of sound that targets cognitive functions, he'll be fine."

"You'll never find an alien here," Lucky shouted.

"Unless, the alien is you," she said.

"What? You're nuts!"

"Sorry, this will hurt a bit," she apologised, and opened fire.

Lucky dodged the blast with ease, though it shattered the glass out of every photo on the mantel piece. Then he dodged left, back to the right, and ran upside down along the roof.

He was closing the distance between them and she was forced to step back, firing again and again. She screamed. She blasted out the windows, tore a hole in the couch and she just managed to graze Lucky's hand.

He was about to grab her when suddenly a pair of strong hands griped his ankles and threw him backwards. He went crashing into the shattered television. The crazy lady took a moment to reconfigure her device.

"Obi, stop!" she ordered. "Now I *know* the alien has been here, and I'd even cut you apart just to prove it! The SRAD

---

[48] Short Range Acoustic Device: A hypothetical weapon that uses sound to disable cognitive functions. Sounds like science fiction? <u>Maybe</u>... just maybe...

Mini can knock out the strongest man alive in a single blast."

It took two blasts to stop him.

***

Chase felt it before he saw it.

They had just gotten home and Arren was walking towards the outer hatch of her spaceship when his heart skipped a beat. He was beginning to wonder what was happening then he realised he was sweating. He was nervous. Then he *felt* nervous. It was a weird sensation.

"Hey, Arren." he laughed. "You'll never guess what just ... Arren?"

She was not moving. She was standing there, like she was completely frozen.

Then Chase realised the entire ship was silent.

Eerily silent. Not a sound. Usually there were squeak of metal doors or clattering of the service spiders from somewhere, but now it was completely silent.

"Arren?" he said.

Suddenly she turned to him, her eyes glowing black, her usual friendly smile replaced with a dispassionate visage. "Evict any humans on board," her voice said, but her mouth didn't move. It came from everywhere on the ship.

Before he could move, she picked him up like a doll and threw him at the door. At the last second it opened and he tumbled out into the living room.

"Arren, what are you –" he started to say, then he realised he was looking right down the barrel of a dangerous looking handgun, except it had a pair of outwards facing cones on the end, like a mini trumpet of evil.

It was being held by a trembling woman in her mid-twenties, dressed in a messy lab coat and wearing a bike helmet coated with foil. At her side a large orange monkey hooted in alarm, a wireless keyboard slung around its neck.

"Time to die, aliens."

***

The other little boy was looking right down the barrel of her SRAD. She didn't take her eyes off him this time. After her experience with the other partially morphed human, she was very wary, and slightly afraid. No-one had ever survived a direct blast, and he had taken two.

"I'm, I'm human," the boy stuttered.

"For now," she replied, only briefly wondering how he could know that it mattered. Keeping the gun pointed right at him, the scientist fumbled for her rod and scanned him from head to foot. Obi-jo had taken control of the alien and her spaceship for now, so as long as she could keep this boy silent, she could get to work.

But just like the other boy, this one had so little alien matter that he was not going to be a problem. It was the girl she wanted.

"You're still much less than one percent changed, boy. I'm doing you a favour here. I'm saving you and everyone in this world from this alien. I need her for my research -"

"She's my friend," the boy argued.

It confused her. Had the alien's tactics changed so much that now they were attempting to befriend some humans? It must have been to infiltrate society, or infect it with their alien ideas. They were disgusting. Had they no limits to their depravity? They had to be stopped.

"Please, please don't take her away. Let her go, she will tell you. Let her go," the boy begged.

He looked so sincere that she almost did consider it. But then she remembered that he was already partially alien. It must have been trying to use the poor boy to stop her.

She's the only alien in there, Obi-jo signed. *Hurry up, we need to get away.*

Besides, if they took the alien away maybe the poor boys would return to normal. Suddenly a black car screeched to a halt in front of the driveway, another turned the corner down the road so fast it almost tipped over.

"Time to go," she agreed. And pointing the gun at the partially transformed human boy on the verge of tears, she backed away into the strange door that was a spaceship.

Chapter 13
Battle for Arrendrallendriania

Chase dodged right. He dodged right because he knew what was about to happen just before it did; Costa kicked the door down in a single move.

He burst in looking just as angry as he did the night Lucky took on the Coebri pirate Lord Tzaarkh: Arren's 'father'. Costa had his gun out. He had his glowing green and ethereal attachment set up and pointed it at the closed spaceship door that was already melting through the living room wall.

"Don't," Chase shouted in desperation. "You'll hurt Arren!"

"Come back!" Costa shouted, and shot the door three times.

Chase covered his face in sympathy. Costa had just shot Arren, shot her three times.

He started to get angry, an insane rage building inside him, when he heard Lucky groan. Chase turned in fright and finally noticed the entire living room was trashed. Every photo, ornament and oil burner shattered. The couch looking like a tiger had taken to sharpening its claws on it.

"Where'd she go?" Costa shouted, grabbing Chase, "What's she up to?"

"I don't know," Chase shouted back in tears, "someone took her."

"Who?" Costa yelled as two more men in black suits, armed with guns, arrived.

"I don't know," Chase replied, "some crazy scientist lady with black hair. I've never seen her before. At least, I don't think I've ever seen her before."

Costa dropped him and whipped out the scanning device.

Chase crawled over to Lucky. He was alive, but stunned. His face was beginning to bruise. Whatever the scientist lady had done, it must have been awful.

"Is Dad all right?" Lucky muttered.

"Dad!" Chase shouted.

"Here," Costa replied. He seemed to have finished shouting at people for now. "Been hit with a stun device, he'll be right."

They stumbled over to Dad and pulled him to his feet. He looked groggily at his dishevelled house. "What do we do now?" he said, not seeming to mind the federal agents who had burst in through the doors.

"We'll need help with this one," Costa muttered.

"Take us," Lucky shouted, then wobbled like he might fall over. "Whoa, what was in that stuff?"

"I don't think you're in any condition to come with us," Flannigan said, looking serious for, well, the first time ever.

"We'll see about that," Lucky said, standing firmly on his feet.

"You'll never get her back without us." Chase turned to Costa and argued, "you know that."

Costa clenched his jaw then hustled them out to the black car while the other men helped Dad. Before they'd even had time to get their seatbelts on, Flannigan hit the accelerator. Lights and sirens popped out of the roof of the car and they were off at breakneck speed.

"Bit faster this time, eh, Lucky?" Flannigan smiled at them both from the driver's seat.

In what must have been less than fifteen minutes they were at the research facility in the city where Mum worked. Costa headed right for the basement, pushing all the security guards aside like he was royalty; they couldn't open doors fast enough for him.

They finally arrived at an elevator, a woman with dark hair was waiting for them. With a sign of relief, Chase saw it was his mother. She was waiting for them with two suitcases and armoured jackets.

Costa began to speak but she cut him off. "Suit up and get in. The boys are coming with us."

Everyone did what she said. Costa and Flannigan joined Chase and his brother, Lucky, in the elevator with Elizabeth, their mum.

She hit the intercom. "Four to see the Mechaniser," she ordered.

There was a pause.

"Maybe he's not ready to be disturbed at this hour?" Flannigan smiled.

"Shut up," Costa replied.

There was a strange jolt. To Chase it felt like all the molecules in his body had been squeezed together for just a moment. He felt a little dizzy.

"What was that?" he asked.

"What? Smoother ride when your girl does it?" Flannigan joked.

"She's not 'my girl'," Chase replied.

"What? No, the female," Flannigan teased. "Oh, you thought I meant girlfriend. Now why would you think that?" The doors opened. "No, this was tunnelling[49]. Whole elevator jumps through space ..."

---

[49] Quantum tunnelling, first described around 1926 by German physicist Fredrich Hund, has a weird name because it doesn't actually involve any tunnels. The idea is that every particle (and maybe even groups of atoms) have many places that they can be in at any one time, which is expressed mathematically by a wave. If the wave is large the particle can actually be found in very different places – even on different sides of an otherwise impassable barrier. So, theoretically, if the wave is made to stretch out, the particles can appear anywhere on that wave, even if that wave is somehow made to stretch across the vastness of space – which is simply science fiction for now. This process has been used to explain how atoms with the same

He probably said more, but Chase didn't hear. They were somewhere else. It looked just like a manufacturing yard inside a cave but all the gear floated about on its own or tumbled across the floor all by itself. There were little crates on wheels that bumped into each other and twisting levers that didn't appear to serve any purpose. There was even a pair of clawed welders that seemed to be arguing over how to mend a table, a table that kept on trying to jump out of the way. Wires, pullies and machines were everywhere.

"Wow, this is ..." Chase began.

Everything stopped. Suddenly the myriad of machines began to pull together, snapping and welding onto each other until they began to form an enormous octopus-like shape with a human-like head. The face was as large as a whole person, made completely from spare parts, chunks of equipment and missing tools. It glowered over them with a terrifying stare.

"WHO DISTURBS THE MEDITATIONS OF THE MECHANIZSER?" it roared.

"Cut it out," Mum said, unimpressed.

"Aww," the enormous mechanical face whined, "it's so much fun when you meet them for the first time, why'd you go spoiling it for me?"

Flannigan laughed. "I was impressed."

Costa glared at him like he was an idiot. "Look, Mechaniser, we don't have time for your games. We and these boys here are after a stolen class two research and reclamation vessel. By the terms of your agreement, you're required to give us access to the glass car."

The giant octopus just sat there for a moment, like it was considering things. When it spoke it bent down,

---

charge, which means they push each other away, still manage to fuse together inside the sun. They 'tunnel' past the barrier and collide into each other.

millions of unoiled gears shrieking in protest, and spoke softly. "I knew she was here but I'm so busy nowadays with all the projects these 'allies' get me on that we haven't really had a chance to say much more than hi. What happened?"

Costa clenched his fists and looked like he was going to say something insulting, but Chase held up his hand. Something told him that he needed this machine's trust more than its obedience.

"Some kind of mad scientist took her. We don't know how or where," Chase told the living machine

The Mechaniser looked regretful. "I should have warned her. Nasty place, this world, at times. Keeps you on your toes. Kept me on my toes ever since I came here four hundred years ago ..." he mused with a melancholy sigh.

"What are you?" Lucky asked.

"I, sir, and am a class *four* research and reclamation vessel. I'd been sent into retirement by the Pyrith that many years ago, after they ascended. Then I found my way to Earth, mostly for the entertainment."

"Class four?" Chase wondered.

"You know your friend is the most advanced robotic life form on this world. Her computing power is so great it makes the entire collaboration of Earth supercomputers look like stone tools next to a stealth bomber! So ..." he looked sad, "so she didn't have anything to say to me."

"Please," Chase begged, "we need to get her back. She could be in great danger. I need her back."

The Mechaniser's frown deepened. "You know she's just a machine," he said, like she could just be put back together, or rebuilt if she didn't turn out right.

Chase felt incensed at the thought and his face must have shown it because the Mechaniser drew back, looking surprised. "But, be that as it may, feel free to help yourself to my glass car. These two alliance agents are capable of piloting it and my other toys."

A mechanised tentacle pulled aside a large sheet which fell away to reveal another spaceship. It like a huge sphere made entirely of glass. It opened up and a swirl of clear stone exposed a short ramp.

"Let's go!" Mum said, and Costa grabbed the bags.

"Take care of her!" the Mechaniser called.

"Please, it's us," Flannigan said with a grin.

"Then take care of *yourselves*," the Mechaniser muttered.

Flannigan had the controls going in moments. The ship began to phase with the ceiling and then floated right through it.

"Cool, just like Arren does," Lucky noted.

"Not at all, I'm afraid," Mum replied, "The Mechaniser is a vastly inferior make to your friend. This craft cannot travel outside a planetary atmosphere and has countless other limitations which we are unable to overcome at our current level of understanding."

"But it does have one advantage," Flannigan muttered, "it can go very, very fast."

And with that, he took off over the city landscape in seconds.

***

The scientist didn't realise how much she was laughing with glee.

The alien and her spaceship was hers, all hers! The topography of the ship was strange, to be sure, and it took her a moment to realise they were, indeed, dealing with a multidimensional craft.

Even so, there was work to be done.

"Obi, instruct the alien to get us back to the lab. We need to pick up our gear," she said.

Won't take a moment, Obi-jo signed, *I've been studying this creature's abilities, it seems we can phase right into the lab and start working without even leaving this ship!*

"Amazing!" the scientist agreed, "now ask this spaceship to get us where we can properly begin the dissection."

***

"There," Mum said. "Right there."

"An apartment right next to the research facility?" Costa mumbled.

"Right under our noses," Mum replied, clenching her teeth.

"Come on," Chase urged them. "We need to get Arren, soon!"

They landed the glass craft on the grass. Costa and Flannigan donned their high tech glasses. Then they armed their guns in spite of Chase's protests and slipped into the building like a pair of spies. Chase and Lucky followed them as they worked their way towards the back door where voices could be heard. Chase felt the room would be empty, but he didn't know why.

Costa burst in, Flannigan right behind him, screaming at the top of his lungs for everyone in there to drop everything and hit the floor.

Chase only got a glimpse of what was happening. There was the scientist lady, and next to her the strange little orangutan typing furiously on the odd looking keyboard around its neck. But the worse thing was Arren. She was lying on some kind of operation table surrounded by various probes, needles and scalpels.

And then the whole scene started to vanish.

Costa swore and fired at them but the bullets hit the wall behind them. The scientist grabbed up her wrist-gun and shot back but the thunderous waves of sound passed right through Costa. Then she laughed.

Costa whipped out his multidimensional gun attachment faster than you could think.

"No!" Chase said and held down his gun, "Wait, stop."

But they disappeared anyway.

Costa shoved him away, he might have even shoved him over if his superior officer wasn't there – Chase's mum. "Now look what you –" he began

"They're still here," Chase interrupted.

"What?" Costa asked.

Flannigan, who apparently hadn't been thinking about his gun at all, was fiddling with his glasses. "Microwaves. The ship is still here," he said.

"Wait," Chase said to the scientist he could no longer see, but if his experience was anything to go by, she could see and hear him perfectly. "Don't do this, please. Please don't hurt her. She's my friend. My *best* friend. You'll hurt her. You just can't do that. She builds things, and she's smart. She likes school and jelly beans..."

He paused.

Then they were gone. Chase felt it and Flannigan knew it at the same time.

"We've lost them," Mum said. "Chase, don't ever interfere with my officers again. Costa had them and at least he is prepared to do what is necessary."

Chase's eyes filled with tears. It wasn't the thought of the way they were prepared to hurt people who got in their way. It was the fact that his mother had told him off, and in spite of all the years he found himself quite powerless against the fear that he'd disappointed her, in spite of it all.

"Where are they now?" she asked Flannigan.

He grabbed his suitcase and started fiddling with the touch screen. "Doesn't make any sense," he said, scanning around. "It's as if they aren't … oh no. I don't think they're on earth anymore."

Chapter 14
Kharon

That was close. The scientist thought. *Way too close.*
"Where are we now?" she demanded.
Obi-jo was silent for a moment. *He said she was his friend*, she signed.
"What? How could you believe that lie?" she shrieked. "He's becoming one of them. Don't you see? We'd all be like that if she had her way. Now TELL ME WHERE WE ARE!"
Obi flinched at the harsh words.
We're hiding, she replied, her hands weak and apologetic.

***

"Not on Earth? Very well. Then we need to see the Gatekeeper," Mum concluded.
Costa and Flannigan looked at her at the same time, concern written all over their faces. They clearly did not look forward to meeting the Gatekeeper.
"Who's he?" Lucky asked with a smile when he saw their discomfort.
"A class *three* research and reclamation vessel," Mum replied as they boarded the glass car. "Get us there fast Flannigan," she ordered.
He punched in co-ordinates and they were underway.
"Jellybeans?" Lucky asked Chase after about ten minutes.
"Yeah, didn't you know?" he replied.
"You two sure do spend a lot of time together."
"What? No, we –"

"So, where are we going?" Lucky interrupted.

"Uluru[50]," Chase said in wonder as he looked out the glass car. It was all glass so there were no windows, or perhaps it was more accurate to say it was *all* windows. But there was Ayers rock, right in the middle of Australia, thousands of kilometres[51] from where they'd just left.

"What's out here?" Chase asked.

"You took the long way around, Flannigan," Mum said with disappointment in her voice.

"Sorry, seems to be a prearranged course," he apologised. Less than a minute later they were whizzing towards a large town, Alice Springs. They headed north towards a large airport with one of those huge golf balls that hide scanning devices.

"Must we see this guy again?" Flannigan asked as they floated down through the ground.

"Do you have the payment?" Mum said in reply.

Costa pulled a small gold and silver coin from his suit. "This guy is making a fortune from us," he said.

"Is that real gold?" Lucky said.

Flannigan handed the coin to Lucky, where Chase could also get a better look. It was made of two colours; dim gold rimmed around a silver circle. It had a large number one and the word "Euro" on it.

"Naw, just copper and nickel with a touch of zinc in the 'gold'," Flannigan replied.

"Who are we paying in European coins?" Lucky asked.

---

[50] <u>Uluru</u> is the name of a large sandstone rock near the centre of Australia, sometimes called Ayers rock. The rock and its surrounding environment are an important location of great religious significance for the local Anangu people.

[51] How far? Over 2,000 kilometres as the crow flies, or 1,200 miles. If it only took them ten minutes to get there, the glass car was travelling at over 15,000 kilometres (9,320 miles) per hour – faster than the fastest passenger airplanes by around 10,000 kilometres per hour!

"A Greek," Mum replied.

When they finally floated down though the rock they came to a dark and mysterious cave. There was a river running through it and at the river's edge a man stood, stooped down underneath his tattered black cloak. They landed the glass car as far away from him as possible.

"Who is it?" Chase asked in a whisper.

"Kharon," Mum said in a matter-of-fact tone.

"Ferryman of the dead," Flannigan replied with a wave of his hand, trying to look quite mystical but really only managing embarrassing.

The air here was cold, as cold and unwelcoming as the dark man on the shore. Chase was sure he knew they were there, but he said nothing as they approached. He found himself wondering if this was the ferryman from the Greek myths that was supposed to take the souls of the dead to the afterlife. Then he found himself wondering how weird all this was; how many alien life forms where scattered all over the Earth, and how many other advanced alien spaceships were mistaken for gods?

"Kharon," Mum said in her business-like tone, "we are in need of your services."

A sound came out of the hood of the cloak with a hiss, and Chase could see a glowing red eye peering at them from its depths.

"I've been waiting for you, Lucky and Chase," the words rolled out like poison.

"Enough, Kharon, we need passage through your portal," Mum ordered.

Kharon turned to face her, slowly, like he had all eternity to wait.

"Forget her, she is a good as *dead*," his wicked voice wheezed.

"Please," Chase began, "you must help us!"

"Oh, I can help you, that's for sure. I felt her leave not a few minutes ago. But where she is now, I cannot send you. Not even I am prepared for a journey such as that. Give her up, boy!"

Chase trembled in anger. "No. I will not."

Kharon laughed. "I felt her the first day she arrived on this *pathetic* orb, streaking from the sky like a toddler taking its first clumsy steps. She has not spoken to me and that is good. I do not like the Coebri, I never will."

"Who are you?" Chase wondered, hoping the information would somehow help him know how to motivate this creature. He seemed to *want* to be unhappy.

"I came to this world over two and a half millennia ago, exiled with the others from my people of Olymnia. I tried to draw a living among the primitive civilisations I found here, living in caves such as this, pandering to their whims for visions and a chance to speak to those they call dead. But I am *tired* of this work. There is little reward in it for me now."

"Then tell me how to get you to save Arren!" Chase demanded.

"Such a big voice for such a little earthling," Kharon laughed, ending in a cough. "I will send you, if only for my own amusement. For where she is now you cannot go."

"Tell us," Chase demanded.

"Venus[52]." Kharon laughed, and it ended in a fit of coughing again. "Even if you went there you would die from the enormous heat and pressure."

---

[52] <u>Venus</u> is the second planet from the sun in our solar system and it's covered with thick clouds. It's about the same size and composition of earth, so for years astronomers thought the thick clouds of Venus could hide huge rainforests similar to Earth. They were wrong. The clouds are made of sulphuric acid, and the runaway greenhouse effect makes the air mostly toxic carbon dioxide. The air is so thick it traps almost all the heat inside, making Venus around 500ºC all day and all night – hot enough to melt some metals.

Chase's heat sank. So the scientist had run somewhere that they couldn't go.

"Surely that glass ball can survive the pressure on Venus," Lucky said.

"That it can," Kharon said with a smile, "but not for long."

"Then we shift out at soon as we get there," Flannigan suggested.

Kharon looked annoyed, then smiled again. "Maybe so, but there is another problem you have not considered. You cannot cross this portal while you are shifted. You must actually arrive on Venus and then face the real problem: the heat. The enormous heat of Venus, five hundred degrees centigrade all day, and all night! Even if you were only there for a few seconds, the heat is so intense it will eventually transfer right through your precious glass and bake you all alive!"

"Why don't we take the portal to the top of the atmosphere?" Lucky asked.

"Fool, do you have any idea how large a planet is?" Kharon mocked. "It'll take you too long to descend through the atmosphere even at your impressive speed. Do you know how long you have? Do you think her captor will not sense you, and flee once more long before you arrive? I can take you right to the ship, right in arms reach if you give me long enough to transpose the co-ordinates, perhaps ... if you gave me access to your GPS satellites it would help ..." he offered to Mum.

"Never happening Kharon; you and your other avatars will not leave these caves."

Hurricane force winds tear at the tops of the clouds while at the surface the air pressure alone is as strong as a kilometre down in the ocean on earth. The sky is always dark, and the lightning never ceases. The entire planet is covered with active volcanoes. Instead of being a forested paradise, Venus may well be the least liveable planet in the entire solar system!

He clenched his fists in frustration. "Bah! Then I may do my best, but you still need a way to survive the heat.[53]"

"The shoebox," Chase suddenly realised. "It's all in the shoebox!"

"What?" Kharon wheezed.

"Look, keeping ice cold in a shoe box is similar to keeping us alive in a space ship on Venus. As soon as we arrive anything we touch will be five hundred degrees hotter than we are. The heat will begin to transfer right to the ship. So if we coat ourselves with something thick with lots of insulation, we'll be right for a little while at least. Then we can lose our coating when we shift over."

"Very clever," Kharon smiled. "But have you thought about everything?"

"Well, then there's the radiant heat. I don't know what we can use to protect ourselves from the heat and infrared energy. We could try wrapping some foil around the spaceship."

Kharon laughed. "That would work right up until the nearby air melted it, which I would expect would take, say, less than half a second."

"Or unless the metal coating was really thick," Costa suggested.

"Hey, I know a guy that had loads of coins just lying around," Flannigan said like he was teasing Kharon.

"NEVER! How DARE you propose to take my income –"

"Kidding, kidding!"

"Wait a minute," Mum said. "Why are we worried about infrared radiation? As long as the rest of our coating isn't see-through and is thick enough, there is no way any radiant heat will be getting in and, unless there is a problem, Flannigan will have us shifted before the heat gets to us."

---

[53] Any thoughts?

"No problem," Flannigan said, winking.

"Good, yes," Chase thought. "Then, there are the convection currents. The air will cool down around the space ship, fall down and be replaced by more hot air from above. But I think the coating will take care of that as well, as long as we're not there for very long."

Kharon was silent. He seemed defeated.

"Every minute you make us wait she comes closer to death," Chase said, not sure whether he was motivated by anger or fear right now.

"Lucky her," Kharon muttered.

Chase found him was weird, and icky.

"Right," Mum shouted, flicking the coin at the robed machine. "Here's your payment Kharon, you know what to do. Everyone else, back in the glass car!"

Kharon took the money with a snarl but got straight to work. Chase looked out from the glass orb as it sunk into the soil and was soon covered with a thick coating of dirt on every side that clung to it like magnetism, or something. Kharon's portal was rising up from the river. It was a grotesque half mechanical dog as large as a bus, with three heads that bit and snapped at each other as it walked onto the shore. Eventually they took hold and their three mouths opened up in a weird circular fashion to reveal a sparkling portal of scintillating blackness between them. The dog continued to open up more and more, until it was a perfect circle standing on the bank of the river.

"Remember," Kharon's voice teased over the intercom that was in their ship, "shift out as soon as you arrive or prepare to enjoy the oblivion of perfect silence." He laughed, and sounded just like he knew something they didn't. "And do come again and see me soon boys, I look forward to our next chat."

Chapter 15
Venus

The scientist paused.

They were on Venus. Finally, there was no way the annoying federal agents who'd somehow caught up to her again could ever follow her all the way out here. She and Obi-jo looked out at the landscape through one of the strange computer screens. She didn't realise just how beautiful it was until her eyes adjusted to the dim red light. The sky was so thick it made the horizon appear to curve upwards no matter where she looked. The air was hot and there were slow flowing rivers of what looked like lava. And far in the distance, the lightning never stopped.

Exceptional.

It was Obi-jo's gentle hoot that brought her back to the situation at hand.

She was standing over the alien, the sharpest surgical knife she had poised in her hand. She was ready to make the first incision to discover what this alien was really made of. She was ready to do to them what they had done to her, though she had no way of stitching things back up so that it didn't make a scar. For a brief, frail moment she wondered if this alien that looked just like a little teenage girl felt any pain.

Suddenly Obi-jo screeched in alarm. *They found us!*

***

Chase screamed.

The scientist was standing over Arren who was on the surgical bed that she had used to recover last time. The scientist had a knife in her hand and Arren was dressed in some kind of surgical outfit. It was obvious what was about to happen.

Costa started firing but his bullets burst against an energy field around the table. Everyone just stood there for a moment.

They were both shifted here, two spaceships occupying the same location but different dimensions. They could see each other, they could hear each other, but unless they synchronised space, they couldn't touch each other. And if either of them shifted back into normal space they'd bake in the hot Venusian environment.

The scientist looked at them. "Elizabeth?"

Mum nodded then spoke, her voice a powerful order. "Melyssa, this is not appropriate, stop your actions at once."

"You!" she almost dropped her knife. "You knew I wasn't lying, didn't you! I told them there were aliens but no-one believed me. But you knew, didn't you! And now I've got one here and we're going to show the world."

"We will do no such thing," Mum said.

The scientist, named Melyssa, looked angry. "Don't try and stop me, Elizabeth. You could have stood up for me back then, you could have stopped them–"

"*Stop* this, Melyssa. This life form is under our protection and we will not treat her this way–"

"We?" Melyssa shot back. Chase could tell his mother was insulting and isolating this crazy scientist with everything she said. And he could tell his mother had no idea. "We? I thought it was me alone when I lost tenure! It's just me! Me and this orangutan."

"Don't," Mum ordered. "You must stop this. I order you to stop this!"

"Stop?" Melyssa yelled. "They took me when I was only a child. No-one stopped them then!"

There was a pause. "Wait, who took you?" Flannigan asked.

"Aliens, aliens like this one," the scientist said, pointing to Arren with her knife.

"Hmm," Mum muttered, "unlikely. As disreputable as the Coebri are, they are not the kind to abduct."

"Sounds more like the Abyleth," Costa offered.

"Yes, we seem unable to keep them from our world in spite of various threats. They are a genetically modified species that have lost their civility generations ago. They plunder across the universe looking for planets outside the Universal Unity for their genetic research. They are small and grey skinned with huge black eyes – the classical alien look."

The scientist stumbled, looking shocked.

"Then I ... this ..." she said, struggling for words.

But Chase could almost see the darkness before it showed on her face, she was going ahead with her plans whether or not Arren was innocent.

"No!" the scientist screamed. "No, it's just another alien, just like all of them. I'm going to cut her up and show the whole world what they are. Then they will listen to me!"

And with a wild sweep of her knife, she cut Arren from her navel to chest. Arren winced but did not move.

Chase felt himself screaming and couldn't hear what anyone else was saying. Then he realised his screams were being drowned out by the orangutan's.

The gruesome table with its dissection was floating closer and closer to them.

The scientist looked puzzled. As if something inside Arren was unexpected.

Chase looked down without even thinking. Everything inside Arren looked just like a person should, except some of the organs glowed with a strange light and he could see her insides pulsed with a rapid, panicked heartbeat.

"It's ... like normal ..." the scientist began. Then she started floating through the floor of her ship even as it started to lift off. "What's happening!"

"Grab her, she's shifting in here!" Costa shouted.

The scientist tried to clutch at Arren, only to find her hands pass right through. Costa leapt towards the scientist but at the last moment she whipped out her weapon and shot him right in the chest. He fell back against the far end of the glass car and didn't get up.

"Obi, what are you doing?" the scientist screamed.

The great ape was screeching something in reply, typing furiously.

The scientist turned the weapon on Flannigan but Lucky was too quick and pushed him out the way. Then Lucky dodged and jumped, leaping off the wall and grabbed the weapon right out of the scientist's hands. Flannigan had her downed and cuffed in a second.

She started crying. "Obi-jo, why? Why did you betray me?"

Mum bent down and calmly jabbed a needle right into Costa's chest. A second later he coughed and started moving again.

"Melyssa, you are under–" Mum started.

"Forget that, where is the orangutan going with Arren?" Chase screamed.

Flannigan lit up a screen just as the image of the operating table vanished entirely. Somehow he'd gotten a connection right into the medical room where the orangutan was screaming and moving its hands in frantic gestures.

"What is she trying to say?" Flannigan wondered.

"I can help you," Melyssa said, "its sign language."

Mum nodded and hauled the handcuffed scientist over while Costa stumbled to his feet, trying to reassess the situation.

"She's really mad," Melyssa the mad scientist said, and paused for a moment before she began to tear up again. "She says it's all my fault, that I was obsessed and blind. That this creature was innocent … she says she's going to take the alien away and make her her best friend forever."

"Not on my watch," Mum said and pushed Flannigan away. "Now you listen here young orangutan. I am well aware of Melyssa's research regarding human simian-intelligence. You are just as valuable an addition to Earth's diverse research programs as-"

Obi-jo screamed in frustration and bared her fangs. Mum flinched, and shut up. Then Obi-jo started typing again.

Somehow, Chase knew what she was about to do. "She is going to cut us off. She is planning to take Arren away."

"What? Why?" Flannigan said.

"She is going to take her away forever, to punish a world that never understood her."

"How do you know that?" Costa demanded.

"He does," Lucky said. "Don't you see? That's what Arren did to him. Like how she changed me. It's true, isn't it Chase. You've been doing it ever since we met her. You can read other people's feelings."

It was like getting hit in the face with a brick. Chase realised that Lucky was right. He'd been guessing what people were thinking and feeling at the school council. He'd known the scientist was dangerous without hearing her say a word.

He promised himself right there and then that he'd be listening in to his feelings a little closer from now on.

Mum was still trying to reason with the orangutan but Chase put his hand on her shoulder. Her feelings were still so far away, yet he could feel she was angry, frustrated that she was fighting a battle she didn't know how to win. With one look in his eyes she stopped and got out of the communication chair.

"Obi-jo," Chase started, not having a clue about what he was going to say, "I know what you're feeling."

The orangutan shouted.

"She doesn't believe you," Melyssa stated the obvious.

"Yes. I know," Chase replied. "But I do, Obi-jo. You feel like an experiment. You are an experiment that everyone used for their own ends while no-one ever asked you about how you *felt*." He couldn't help but tear up, feeling just how lonely this creature had felt for all these years. "So clever, but once the novelty wore off they forgot you, leaving you with a scientist who didn't really understand you, who just used you as a tool."

"I never ..." Melyssa began, but a few frantic gestures from Obi-jo convinced her that Chase was saying exactly how she felt.

"But Obi-jo, Arren is my friend. My best friend. She ran away from her people because they wanted to make her a slave. She hid with my family so that she didn't become an experiment. Please. Please don't take her away from us."

Obi-jo stopped.

"Her name is Arren," he said.

The orangutan started making strange sounds, like sobbing.

"Let her go," Chase asked, "let her repair herself. Then you will see, see she is one of the best friends you could ever wish for."

Melyssa translated what the orangutan signed, "If you love something, set it free ..."

Obi-jo typed a single command on her control panel, and Arren screamed. Bright flashes of lightning streaked across the medical floor and it looked like the orangutan was thrown clear across the room.

When the dust cleared Arren was standing up, eyes returning to normal from glowing a brilliant white. She was holding the gown across her chest but a large, nasty scar ran from under her hand, down towards her stomach.

"I'm OK," she smiled.

Everyone breathed a sigh of relief.

"Melyssa, you are under arrest for abduction and grievous physical harm to a minor," Costa was saying.

"Wait," Chase said. He could feel the defeat and despair welling up inside the confused and distraught scientist.

"*Unthinkable*," Mum replied. "We have our due process to attend to. Those that steal aliens in our care must be subjected to the full force of the law."

Chase heard Obi-jo hooting softly from inside Arren's spaceship. He knew what she was thinking. He knew the orangutan could never face the same punishment. She was never coming back to earth again while her scientist friend faced merciless justice and a life in jail.

"Mum, please," Chase said.

"Yeah, Mum, have a heart," Lucky agreed. He wanted the scientist set free too. Chase could see, he thought she was cute, even if she was probably six years older than him. Had he already forgotten that she had cut up Arren!

"Ethylmetholtrethadine," Arren suddenly said.

"What?" Mum and Flannigan chorused.

"I have detected considerable amounts of Ethylmetholtrethadine in your blood stream, Ms Chase and Lucky."

"Impossible, what would that powerful neurostimulant be doing in my bloodstream?" she demanded.

Arren said nothing.

"Maybe someone's been tampering with your medicine," Lucky suggested.

Chase had to wonder, how would Lucky have guessed that? He wasn't on the excursion to scan Mum.

Perhaps Chase just wasn't the only one with a little intuition after all …

Chapter 16
Ice in a Box

It was the day of the long awaited ice in a shoe box competition. It was always a term long project but as Chase looked at their entry, he knew he'd win. Not everyone had experienced keeping alive on Venus as preparation! The box was lined with polystyrene, resting on a cold stone floor, painted black inside and coated with the same blue lined foil they used in housing on the outside. There wasn't a single gap for air to move in, out, or around. Arren had even added a little double glazed window from an old oven they'd found lying around Ms Garibaldi's yard. It was the winning entry, for sure!

Arren yawned.

"Mum still keeping you up?" Lucky grinned.

She nodded, and smiled. "Last night was probably the toughest. She can't sleep and every feeling and issue pushed under by a psychotropic medicine for over eight years just comes gushing out time after time. She's taken to sitting in her old room or the back yard while I pat her on the back and say 'there, there'."

"That's rough," Lucky said.

It was. Chase kept on having to leave the house while she went on her bouts of emotional release, coming down the hard way off the illegal dosage. Any little thing set her off, from having two cups the same colour on the sink to watching a leaf fall in the back yard. She hadn't moved back in, but she'd been there all weekend since she'd decided rehab wasn't helping anymore, and she needed something like a family.

It had been a tough weekend.

"Reckon they'll find out who did it?" Chase wondered.

"No, not any time soon," Arren said. "She let me read the official investigation but they have no idea who managed to tamper with her medicine."

It made Chase angry but there was nothing he could do about it now. At least it was a start; at least they might begin to put their family back together, maybe.

"How about you Arren," Lucky asked. "What are you going to do now Mum's thrown you out of her bedroom and Dad's sleeping on the couch?"

She smiled. "Don't worry about me. I've got a plan. You know the laundry cupboard? I'm going to set up a portal in my spaceship so that when you turn the cupboard handle to the *left* instead of *right* it'll lead right to my entry dock. Pretty cool, eh? I'll miss sleeping on Earth but we won't be getting in the way!"

"Yeah, probably safer that way anyway," Chase agreed. He knew what she meant by 'we'; Obi-jo was hiding inside Arren's spaceship, no doubt studying alien computer systems from the comfort of the indoor garden. Apparently she also had quite the talent for chess, but Chase almost never saw the little ape.

He still couldn't get the image of the scientist out of his head, nor the sight of the great scar that ran right down Arren's front. Even though it had healed so well it was almost invisible now, he knew it would never heal completely.

The mood in the room suddenly changed. He felt it before he saw it. He was getting better at catching other people's feelings. Most of the time he didn't notice except when someone was having a particularly strong feeling, which at times was pretty embarrassing. It turned out teachers had feelings too, some were very powerful – something he'd never even thought about.

And right now someone was feeling pretty darn smug about themselves: It was Mark T. He walked in victoriously carrying his shoebox lined with copious amounts of aluminium foil. There was no actual way in; a door was drawn on the side.

And behind him a huge hulk of a man walked in with a large container: a red, pudgy man with a squinty face and ready smirk. He looked like a truckie, with a red goatee and moustache, thick muscly arms and a bulging stomach that would have rested over the steering wheel while he drove. Chase didn't even need to examine his emotions to recognise the family similarity – it was Mark T's notorious dad.

"Get back, get back!" he yelled at people, crashing his large container on the ground in the covered area just outside the classroom where the contest was happening.

Mark stood on a chair and opened up his shoebox, beginning a prepared speech. "Good evening all! This is *our* entry to the insulated shoebox competition. Now, I've discovered a neat little trick to keeping a house cool. Some houses are built *into the ground* to keep themselves insulated. The ground acts as a heat sink to keep the house cool," he explained with a generous wave of his hands. "Also, many cultures have used blocks of ice to help their places stay cool. Some blocks of ice buried in underground cellars can keep frozen all summer and so help preserve the food. So, in respect to these *actual innovations* to keeping the house cool, I've prepared *this!*"

His dad opened the container and pulled out a shoebox sized slab of granite about the same thickness of his big beefy hand. It was steaming with cold.

"Liquid nitrogen!" Arren cried in dismay.

"Yes, in respect to the ancient technologies I've added a little modern innovation! A cold rock that will keep this ice freezing for hours!"

"But, sir," Arren complained.

The teacher was thinking. "Actually, I quite like the idea. It's innovative and it draws on available materials very well."

"But you can't keep a house cool with liquid nitrogen!" Chase argued.

"I've heard of it happening[54]," he disagreed.

"But sir," Lucky pled.

They watched in dismay as the contest began.

Mark T won by a long shot. His ice was still frozen by the time all the others' had melted. His ice was still frozen by the time school ended, covered with a snowy coating of condensed ice. His ice, the teacher informed them, was still floating around by the time he arrived the next day.

Everyone clapped when the visiting council member shook Mark's hand in assembly.

Everyone, except Lucky, Arren and Chase.

Arren clenched her teeth. "I cannot believe we lost a science contest to Mark T!" she almost screamed.

"That's just because he cheated," Lucky said. "Teacher's probably just scared of Mark's dad."

Chase thought about that. "No, he wasn't. I think he wanted Mark to experience winning something without cheating." He offered a few polite claps as well. "But I still don't understand why the teacher offered such poor descriptions of how to win the contest, we didn't know we could use cold rocks."

"I totally agree, oh, it makes me so *angry!*" Arren said.

Lucky laughed, and Chase smiled.

Then, slowly, something he didn't really want to realise pushed itself to the front of his mind. Arren *said* she felt angry, she clenched her teeth and fists and *looked* a little angry, but Arren didn't *feel* it. Chase had no idea what she

---

[54] I haven't. I don't know where this guy gets his information!

was feeling unless she told him. Because of the power she'd given him he could tell what anyone was feeling when he was speaking to them. He could tell what his friends were feeling across the room. He could tell what his brother was feeling just about anywhere. But Arren was as mysterious as girls had ever been. Even his mother had had more feelings to feel than Arren.

It was then, even more than looking at her burn with fire, or see the scintillating colours she said was her computer. Even more than seeing her cut open with a knife and standing healed in the next moment.

Chase finally began to realise his friend Arren … really *wasn't* human …

And suddenly he felt very, very nervous …

About the author

Dr Joe (AKA Dr Joseph Ireland) is a science educational specialist operating out of Brisbane, Australia. He has a wife, three daughters, and two pet mice who help him with his Magic of Science shows. He enjoys playing Dungeons & Dragons with friends and has written award winning fiction for the Living Greyhawk series. His true passion is in understanding and promoting scientific ways of thinking in society, having lectured in Science, Technology and Society at Queensland University of Technology.

If you're looking for an exciting science show for your school why not visit www.DrJoe.id.au to find out more!

Elizabeth is the second book in the series *Space Chase*, which explores sound scientific concepts within the framework of an engaging science fiction narrative. This story focuses on heat, states of matter, and coloured fire! We also clarify the relationships between Lucky, Chase and their strange, and estranged, parents. Elizabeth is a compelling and informative narrative designed to make science fiction, and science fact, fun!

Buy your own copy at www.DrJoe.id.au!

Space Chase - Elizabeth

Place your mark here each time you read this book!

Feedback and comments are always welcome Arren@drjoe.id.au

www.ingramcontent.com/pod-product-compliance
Lightning Source LLC
Chambersburg PA
CBHW050315010526
44107CB00055B/2254